Tips & Traps
for Hiring a Contractor

Tips & Traps
for Hiring a Contractor

R. Dodge Woodson

McGRAW-HILL

New York   Chicago   San Francisco   Lisbon   London
Madrid   Mexico City   Milan   New Delhi   San Juan
Seoul   Singapore   Sydney   Toronto

The McGraw·Hill Companies

Cataloging-in-Publication Data is on file with the Library of Congress

1 2 3 4 5 6 7 8 9 0   DOC/DOC   0 1 0 9 8 7 6 5

ISBN 0-07-144584-6

The sponsoring editor for this book was Cary Sullivan and the production supervisor was Pamela A. Pelton. It was set in Garamond by Lone Wolf Enterprises, Ltd. The art director for the cover was Handel Low.

Printed and bound by RR Donnelley.

Interior clipart images courtesy of www.clipart.com.

McGraw-Hill books are available at special quantity discounts to use as premiums and sales promotions, or for use in corporate training programs. For more information, please write to the Director of Special Sales, McGraw-Hill Professional, Two Penn Plaza, New York, NY 10121-2298. Or contact your local bookstore.

 This book is printed on recycled, acid-free paper containing a minimum of 50% recycled, de-inked fiber.

Dedication

I dedicate this book to Adam and Afton, the two best children a father could ask for. Afton has supported my writing since my first book, and Adam has never complained about my need to finish a chapter before venturing into our woods. They truly are the best children I could have dreamed of.

Contents

About the Author

R. Dodge Woodson has been involved in the building trades for 30 years and has been a self-employed contractor for 25 years. He is the owner of The Masters Group, Inc., a general contracting, remodeling, and plumbing firm in Maine. Woodson has written dozens of books on the industry for both consumers and professionals.

Introduction

A re you thinking of hiring a general contractor for home improvements or remodeling? Has the thought of saving thousands of dollars by being your own general contractor crossed your mind? Most homeowners seeking to improve their homes either hire a general contractor or act as their own construction manager while hiring subcontractors. In either case, this book is one of the most important tools that will be found on the job site.

Adding space to your home or improving existing living conditions can be a very traumatic time. But, it doesn't have to be. With the right knowledge, you can maintain control of your job. It will be easier on you to hire a general contractor, but there is a lot of money to be saved if you act as your own general contractor.

Almost anyone researching the rules of the road for remodeling has discovered horror stories about doing business with contractors and subcontractors. These stories are true. R. Dodge Woodson, the author, has been in the business for 30 years. He shares many of his own experiences between these pages. Best of all, he tells readers what to watch out for and how to avoid costly mistakes before, during, and after a home improvement or remodeling job.

Woodson has compiled a career of information here to help and protect you. For the mere cost of this book, you may save thousands of dollars on your job. Even more important, it is likely that you will avert disaster by not making the types of mistakes that many homeowners and inexperienced general contractors make.

Thumb through these pages. Notice the bullet lists, the tip boxes, and the numerous sample forms. The author has taken a serious, complicated subject and turned it into an accessible, easy-to-understand guide for homeowners. The writing is concise and the illustrations point out key factors toward a successful job.

You don't have to be a victim of unscrupulous contractors. Woodson will show you how to avoid them. Additionally, you will learn how to manage reputable contractors and assure yourself of quality work that comes in on budget and on time. Your home may be your single largest investment; don't risk it to renegade contractors. Learn how to protect yourself, your finances, and your home with this reader-friendly roadmap to success.

Go ahead and spend a little time looking over the chapters. It will not take long to see the value of Woodson's invaluable experience and advice. You don't have to go it alone. Take the words of a veteran contractor with you along every step of your remodeling adventure. Pick and choose the topics that you need, but don't go home without this essential element of your new project.

1

Should You Be Your Own Contractor for Home Improvements?

There are projects in life where you can use your talents and experience and others you would never even consider trying. A friend knows of your culinary prowess and asks you to make her wedding cake; no problem. The den needs more shelves, and in a matter of minutes you have completed the task. It's simply a matter of the right tools for the job and a little knowledge of the basics.

Yet, suggest remodeling your house or making home improvements and there are usually just two reactions, "Are you out of your mind!" and "We're not talking a few shelves here, we're talking major work. I can't do that." Just as with the shelf installation, you will find you have experience in remodeling you never knew existed. Organization, patience, and basic product knowledge are all essential elements to any remodeling project. You need only to examine your qualifications and decide if you have the skills required to run your own job. If not, investigate choosing the right person or people for the project. Should you coordinate the work or hire a general contractor? This question will require a lot of thought. The wrong decision can be very expensive and frustrating. Being your own general contractor can save you a lot of money. It can also cost you more than paying professionals to do the work. Before jumping into a quick decision, consider all the factors. A little time spent now can save a lot of time and money later.

There are several types of qualified contractors available. They range from major corporations to individual, one-man firms. The trick is locating and choosing the right contractor for your job. Remodeling is often a complicated process and requires special talents. Matching your needs to the contractor's ability is mandatory for a successful job. There is much more to being a general contractor than hiring a few subcontractors and scheduling the work. If the role of a general contractor was easy, it wouldn't be such a lucrative business.

Remodeling and home improvements vary dramatically from new construction. You will encounter problems and unexpected complications not found in new construction. Many homeowners look immediately to what they perceive to be simple aspects of a remodeling project. They think they can do much of the work themselves to save money. Don't be fooled! Even a simple alteration, like changing the bathroom faucet, can be laborious and plagued with problems. The supply lines could break or crimp, or there may be no water cut-off valves to the faucet. Entire sink tops have been known to break during a routine faucet replacement. There is a difference between

Many homeowners discredit the idea of doing work themselves, but contemplate acting as their own general contractor. This involves more details to consider than just saving a few dollars. It is only with the right personality and ability that these savings become a significant factor. The potential savings are very tempting. The lure of keeping up to 30 percent from coordinating your own project has a strong influence on many consumers. Some homeowners are well suited to the task. If you fall into this category, you are fortunate. Your savings overall should average about 20 percent.

coordinating the changes made by professionals and acting as a tradesman. Only consider doing work yourself in areas were you have specific experience. Keep in mind, if you are using a plumber to replace your bathroom fixtures, you will not save much installing the faucets yourself.

MONEY TO BE SAVED

The percentage of money that can be saved by being your own contractor is based on the total value of the job, not the cost of the work. This is an important detail. There is a sizable difference between the retail value of the improvement and the cost to make the improvement. Your profit will be based on the retail value. An estimated job cost indicates the anticipated cost of completing the job. The value is based on the appraised worth of the completed project.

> It is best to engage a professional appraiser to ascertain the value of large home improvements. A general rule of thumb is, cost plus 20 percent equals value. When you examine your anticipated savings, use retail values.

When you hire a contractor to do home repairs for you, expect the contractor to make a minimum profit of 20 percent of the improvement value. Let's assume the value of your job is $30,000. The general contractor wants this same appraised value for his work. Acting as your own contractor, the job should only cost around $24,000. You could do a lot with the $6,000 savings. However, if you prefer hiring out the work, you should be checking to make sure that your contractor is not pocketing more than 20 percent of the total value of the improvement.

The responsibilities of a general contractor are tedious and can be a losing proposition. If the job is not handled properly, money and time will be lost. Before becoming a contractor, consider the consequences carefully.

Questions to Ask Yourself Before Becoming Your Own Contractor

- Will you have time to arrange for blueprints and specifications?

- Will you be available to supervise the work while it's being done?

- Is special insurance needed to protect you from liability?

- Do you have a basic knowledge of the kind of work you are considering, such as the steps involved to replace your bathtub?

- These are just a small example of the questions to be answered.

More Questions To Ask Yourself

- Do you have time to be your own general contractor?

- How much time is required?

- Are you going to be available during the normal working hours?

- Will you be able to make phone calls in the evenings?

- Are you able to leave work for a few hours if necessary?

- Can you afford to take off from work to tend to your home fires?

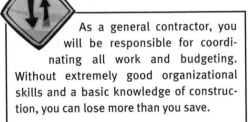

As a general contractor, you will be responsible for coordinating all work and budgeting. Without extremely good organizational skills and a basic knowledge of construction, you can lose more than you save.

The best way to determine your ability is to put the facts on paper. Make a brief outline of your credentials. Explore all of your experience and strong points. Compare the similarities of your abilities to the requirements of a general contractor. Be honest with yourself. It is critical to know if you can actually handle the responsibility of a general contractor. This is your first major decision.

SUBCONTRACTORS

Unfortunately, many subcontractors may not be very dependable. This creates problems for even the most experienced general contractors. These subs can be difficult to motivate, even for a professional with years of experience. As a homeowner, with only one remodeling job, you are likely to find subcontractors difficult (but not impossible) to control. The demands on your personal time must be carefully evaluated. You will spend hours running the job. Much of this time will conflict with your standard work schedule. If you are not at your remodeling job, you don't know if the subs showed up. You won't know about their absence until the evening. By then, you have lost a whole day of production. Your night will be spent calling all the other contractors, because their work will have to be rescheduled. Every trade depends on another trade. When one is out of step, they are all thrown off schedule.

MATERIAL DELIVERIES

Material deliveries come during business hours. Are you able to confirm deliveries from work? Unfortunately, the numerous daytime phone calls required to coordinate your project will be a distraction. Will your job allow enough flexibility to make these calls? They must be made, how will you accomplish the chore? It may be wiser to hire a professional management team or general contractor.

What will you do when your materials don't arrive? The subcontractors are there, but they have no material to work with. The subcontractors are going to request additional

Your regular job can suffer when your time is divided by supervising the remodeling project. Weigh your sacrifices, and don't risk losing your full-time job. The remodeling savings won't justify becoming unemployed. You will need to devote a large portion of your spare time to the remodeling project. Determine what your time is worth.

Depending on your income, you may not save anything by supervising your own job. Consider your hourly income and compare it to the cost of a professional contractor. Don't underestimate the demands for your personal attention. There will be numerous evening phone calls to make, and on-the-job problems will demand your personal attention. This is a decision that you will have to make.

compensation for time lost due to a lack of materials. Material acquisition is the general contractor's responsibility. If you fail to get materials on the job, it will cost you big money. Suppliers are a problem, even for the pros. Can you handle them? What will you do when the cabinets, which were going to take six weeks for delivery, are late?

Your first reaction will be one of anger. You will want to tell the supplier to take a hike, but where can you get the cabinets any quicker? This type of problem is common. You've waited six weeks already. If you change suppliers, you will have to wait even longer. If you rely on the existing supplier, who now promises delivery in two weeks, will you wait two weeks and still not have the cabinets? The supplier did not meet their first delivery date, what guarantee do you have that they will meet this one?

These are tough decisions, even for a seasoned professional. Most contractors will gamble on the two-week delivery. Sometimes they lose and the cabinets still don't show up. The contractor is a prisoner of the supplier. Making the right decision is based on unknown factors. How can you trust suppliers who do not keep their commitments? This dilemma can keep you up at night. All you can do is decide based on experience or gut reaction. There are ways to protect yourself from delivery catastrophes. The point being made here is that these are the types of events involved with supervising your remodeling project.

What Will You Have To Do?

- As a general contractor, you are responsible for everything.
- You will need to produce cost estimates as part of the planning stage for your project.
- If you are applying for financing, you need to know if the lender will accept your estimates.
- Does the lender's policies allow a homeowner to be the general contractor?

- Will the code enforcement office issue you the proper permits?

- Where will you obtain plans and specifications?

- Do you have the available cash to front the expenses of the job?

- Will your experience be adequate to keep the subcontractors honest?

- How much control will you have over the subcontractors?

ESTIMATING

Cost estimating can be tedious. You can read books in an attempt to learn estimating techniques. Some books will tell you what to expect for the cost of various projects. These books can be a good idea, but they are expensive. Their expense must be weighed against the money and time they can save you. A few flaws exist with estimating books. For example, the time requirements and estimates given are not universally accurate. Many of the books base their cost figures on union wages. Very few residential jobs are done by union members. Trade wages can differ by more than five dollars per hour. This factor alone can make a dramatic difference on a large job.

Another fault found in many of these books is the geographical cost differences. Prices in California cannot be compared to the prices in Florida. Maine contractors and suppliers will charge different prices than the same vendors in Virginia. Some companies, like the R.S. Means Company, Inc. of Kingston, Massachusetts, publish a variety of books which include a City Cost Index to allow for geographical differences. The *Means Home Improvement Cost Guide,* and the *Means Repair and Remodeling Cost Data* book are specifically geared to remodeling projects. These types of books will provide you with a rough idea of what to expect. The books are good for use as guides and reference material. They are an excellent educational tool in learning the steps of construction or remodeling.

Certainly, they have value to the uninformed consumer, but don't accept the figures for costs until you adjust for your geographical location.

> Firm quotes from suppliers and contractors provide the best way to estimate your intended job cost. There will be much less room for error in your estimate.

There is an easier way to get accurate figures. This approach won't erode your valuable time and the figures obtained will be reliable. This is the method I used when I first became a general contractor. Firm quotes from suppliers and contractors provide the best way to estimate your intended job cost. There will be much less room for error in your estimate. These quotes will guarantee many of your expenses. Written quotes can even be obtained through the mail. This is a simple process, but you need to know specifically what to ask for. If you already know what you want, you are way ahead of the game. If you don't, do some research. This is where those estimating books can be of the most help.

SPECIFICATIONS

When you embark on a remodeling or improvement project, you will need to invest enough time to create specifications. The specifications must be very specific. Read books, talk to suppliers, look at advertisements. All of this will prepare you for creating clear specifications. When you know exactly what you want, contact the bidders. When you ask a plumber for the price to install your bathroom, the plumber will require details. What brand of fixtures do you want? Do you want copper water distribution pipe, or PEX tubing? If you decide on copper, do you prefer type "M," "L," or "K."? Would you like schedule 40, PVC piping for your DWV system, or do you prefer ABS? What grade fixtures do you want? Fixture options include Competitive, Builder Grade, Standard, and Top-of-the-Line. Will you want your bathtub to be fiberglass, acrylic, steel, or cast iron? How much do you want to spend on your faucets?

Lavatory faucets start at less than twenty dollars and can cost more that $2,000.

Is a 1.6 gallon, water saver toilet suitable for your job? The principal is a good one, but will one and a half gallons of water be sufficient to flush the toilet with your old pipes? Should you have a china lavatory or a cultured marble top? Do you want an oak veneer vanity or a solid wood cabinet? Does it really make a difference? Will particle board delaminate in the bathroom moisture? Had enough of the question bombardment? All right, you get the overall idea.

These are only a few of the decisions a general contractor must make. The questions are determined by your individual situation. For example, should you invest in a temperature control shower valve? It is a very good safety feature if there are young children or elderly members in your family. If you have back problems or elder family members, an 18-inch toilet is a wise investment. Of course, unless you are clairvoyant, you will not know all the questions to ask. Remodeling and home improvement is a step-by-step process. First you will come up with an idea of the changes you want to make. Then you will start to choose the accessories to make those changes a reality. How will you know what questions to ask? The same way a general contractor does. List all of your requirements and desires. Then contact vendors of those products. It can be as simple as asking a plumbing supplier, "Is there any way to protect our children against accidental scalding?".

You will be amazed at the variety and usage of products available. For example, spas and whirlpools offer unlimited opportunities. You can spend $2,000 or $6,000. What is the difference between a spa and a whirlpool? Most people don't know, but you are about to learn. The big difference is that spas are designed to hold water indefinitely. You fill them, treat the water with chemicals, and they are constantly ready for your enjoyment. Whirlpool tubs are meant to be filled with water each time you use them. This can be an expensive form of relaxation. Consider the cost of producing hot water to fill the whirlpool. Many units hold ninety gallons of water, or more. In most residential situations, you will empty your water heater each time the whirlpool is filled. Heating this volume of water consumes a lot of expensive energy. Whirlpools are less expensive, but spas offer more benefits. While on this subject, it is worth mentioning that certain products, such as bubble bath oils, may not be recommended for use with whirlpools and spas. Check the manufacturer's recommendations before putting any additives into your bath or spa water.

Now let's make you a carpeting expert. Carpeting is an easy job for the homeowner to subcontract, right? Not unless you know the keys to the floor covering industry. If you buy an expensive carpet, with an infe-

> If you buy an expensive carpet with an inferior pad, you are making a mistake.

rior pad, you are making a mistake. The pad is the most important part of your floor covering. An inexpensive carpet on a quality pad will last much longer than an expensive carpet on a poor pad. Do you know how to recognize a good carpet or pad? Ask the carpet representative to show you the difference in the available products.

Have them put four sample pads on a floor along with four different grades of carpet. Lay the carpet samples on each pad. Now, with heavy soled shoes, walk on the carpet. Which carpet was the quickest to eliminate your footprints? Make a note of the carpet and have the salesperson move the carpets to different pads. Try the test again. Did the same carpet win? I doubt it. The proof is in the pad. This procedure allows you to determine the difference between carpets and their pads. You can easily evaluate your best value with this procedure.

What knowledge do you have of heating systems? Can you determine the BTUs required to heat your living space? What type of heat will best meet your requirements? You can choose between heat pumps, boilers with tankless coils, electric heat, and forced hot air units. The standard energy sources include, electricity, oil, natural gas, and LP gas. Here is a suggestion. Contact your power and utility companies. Many power companies offer programs designed to save energy and increase your savings. You may find they can answer many of your questions regarding properly heating your improved home. Is natural gas available in you neighborhood? If possible, should you heat your hot water with your home heating system? Will it supply an adequate volume of hot water? Will your existing electrical service accommodate your new improvements? If the utility company doesn't have the answer, try asking the local codes enforcement office.

Other questions are not as easily answered. How many coats of mud will your new drywall require? Do you need to prime or seal your surfaces before painting? What thickness of insulation should you use in your new space? These are all important questions. As a general contractor, you must be able to answer them. Your only hope, if you can't find answers to these questions, is honest subcontractors. Honest subcontractors can be hard to find.

It is unlikely, as a homeowner, you will be fully versed in answering these technical questions. Professional general contractors have many advantages over the average homeowner. Experienced general contractors have dealt with the majority of problems commonly encountered. They know which products are commonly used versus which ones are required. General contractors use subcontractors on a regular basis. They know their subcontractor's faults. Due to the future work available from the contractor, subcontractors will respond quickly to the request of the general. Experienced general contractors know how to handle problems that arise on a daily basis. Successful generals have endured the test of time. They have paid the dues for their experience.

> As a homeowner, you run the risk of losing money as a general contractor. If events go as planned, you will save a bundle. If they don't, you'll lose your shirt. Average homeowners are better off working with a licensed general contractor.

YOUR ABILITIES

How will you determine your abilities? Don't let potential savings taint your judgement. You must address your project objectively. If after thorough evaluation, you feel qualified to tackle the job, do it. Consider all the repercussions before making a final decision; it may be more cost effective to hire a professional remodeling contractor. Your time has value, determine this value and compare it to the cost of a good contractor. At first glance, being a contractor looks easy. This encourages many carpenters to go into the remodeling business to fulfill their dreams of untold riches. Homeowners fall into the same trap. General contracting is not easy, it is hard work and requires special abilities.

Remodeling projects rarely go as planned; the ability to make sound judgement calls is paramount. Don't force yourself into a failing situation which could doom your entire project for the sake of a few dollars.

General contracting is not a fountain of financial freedom. The profession is plagued with uncontrollable circumstances. General contractors are dependent on subcontractors. If the subs don't do their job, the general cannot do his. This is a frustrating and helpless feeling. A homeowner only has one job to offer the subcontractor. If a scheduling conflict arises, the homeowner loses. Subcontractors almost always respond to the people providing their primary income. This is rarely the homeowner. Subcontractors are dependent on general contractors. When a general calls, the sub will respond. This can require stalling a homeowner's job. They must look at their long-term income. A homeowner only has one job to offer, the general contractor has many profitable jobs during the year. As a self-contractor, you will be faced with this problem.

General contractors are in business to make your life easier. You pay them 20 percent of the job's value to take care of the problems. They coordinate everything. When you have a problem or a question, you deal with the general contractor. All of your problems are handled through one source, and this is a strong advantage. Simply contacting all the subcontractors involved in a change order is a time consuming process. Almost any changes made will affect several subcontractors. For instance, the decision to move your vanity farther down the wall will result in numerous phone calls. The first call will be to the plumber. Then, the electrical contractor will need to be contacted to move lights and outlets. The carpenter may need to adjust for the changes.

This simple vanity relocation may affect your ceramic tile design. When the decision is made after drywall is hung, you'll have to contact the drywall contractor. There may even be a conflict with your heating system's location. This example shows the effect of a so-called simple change. For each subcontractor involved, you will spend a lot of time on the phone and on the job site. These situations drain your personal time. A general contractor will handle all these changes after just one phone call from you

The general contractor will coordinate all material deliveries. As a self-contractor, would you be able to handle improper material shipments? What will

> If your time is valuable, a general contractor is a good investment.

happen when the material you were promised for Tuesday still isn't on site by Friday? This means down-time for your craftsmen. They will want reimbursement for lost production time or may leave to do another job. If you are the general contractor, it is your responsibility to provide for and coordinate their work. Once they have left your job, it is unlikely they will come back until their next contract is complete. If you have a full-time, regular job, how will you get these problems resolved? Suppliers are hard to deal with and can be very undependable. They are notorious for broken promises. Paying plumbers to stand around, while you locate their missing material will cost you a small fortune. You can count on this problem arising, there is no way to avoid it. By hiring a general contractor, these headaches become their problem.

Subcontractors can ruin your production schedule. If your heating contractor does not show up, you will have to reschedule your other subs. When the insulator lets you down, you have to rearrange your drywall contractor and painter. Everything that goes wrong creates a chain effect. With a general, the problem still exists, but you don't have to deal with it personally. If you follow the rules you learn in this book, you will have written clauses in the contract to insure your job is completed in a timely manner. The general contractor is the one losing sleep over scheduling problems, not you.

> Subcontractors can ruin your production schedule.

Paying for the work is another advantage to a general contractor. General contractors will frequently bill you. For large jobs this could be on a monthly basis. On the other hand, subcontractors will want payment upon completion of their work. This can be a problem if you are financing the job. Lenders will expect you to pay tradesmen and suppliers before advancing a loan disbursement. Financing presents its own challenges, and is an entirely separate consideration.

What other factors do you need to think about before deciding to be your own general contractor? There is the consideration of protecting yourself and your home. Will you need additional insurance? Acting as your own general contractor may not be covered under your existing insurance. General contractors carry liability insurance to protect you and your property. You should ask for evidence of this insurance before signing any contracts with a general. There are many potential risks which make liability insurance compulsory. What happens if a carpenter drives a nail through your water distribution pipe? Your house floods! Who is responsible for the damage repair? How will you handle an electrician falling through your ceiling? It wouldn't be the first time someone was working in the attic and lost their footing. When using a general contractor, the contractor is responsible to you for these damages. Without a general, will your homeowner's insurance protect you?

Before making a final decision on who will run your project, read the rest of this book. The following chapters hold a wealth of information. Your decision on who should handle the contracting of the job will be easy to make when you are fully informed. It's tempting to try to get by without professional management. I encourage you to take advantage of the opportunity, if you are qualified. Evaluate what you learn from this book and make educated decisions. Take the Contractor Quiz, at the end of this chapter, as a tool in evaluating your potential as a general contractor. The time you spend researching your options will be well rewarded.

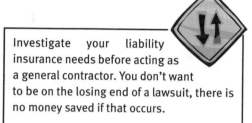

Investigate your liability insurance needs before acting as a general contractor. You don't want to be on the losing end of a lawsuit, there is no money saved if that occurs.

The information here will not protect you from all of the pitfalls of remodeling and home improvements. It would be impossible to anticipate all the potential problems. Even after thirty years as an active remodeler, plumbing contractor and general contractor, I still learn something new with many jobs. While I can't protect you, I can prepare you for the journey into having work done on your home. Your project will run much smoother with the proper knowledge. This knowledge will benefit you as a consumer or a contractor.

For the following questions, rate your answers on a scale of one to ten. On the scale, one is very weak or not at all. Ten is very strong or a definite yes. For example, if the question was,"Do you have a full-time job?," this is how you would answer. Indicate the numeral 10 for a full-time job. Use the number 5 for a part-time job and use number 1 if you don't have a job. If the question was, "Can you make quick, accurate decisions?," this is how you would answer. If you feel strongly that you can, enter the number 10. If you are unsure of your ability, enter a number between 1 and 5. If you have average decision making skills, use the number 5.

ARE YOU READY TO BE YOUR OWN CONTRACTOR?

1.	Rate your ability to supervise your project during the day.	0	5	10
2.	Do you have a full time job?	0	5	10
3.	Do you enjoy working with people?	0	5	10
4.	Do you have strong leadership ability?	0	5	10
5.	Are you comfortable around strangers?	0	5	10
6.	How often do you believe what you are told?	0	5	10
7.	Do you act on impulse without thought?	0	5	10
8.	Are you allergic to dust?	0	5	10
9.	Do loud, repetitive noises bother you?	0	5	10
10.	Does your regular job require you to manage people?	0	5	10
11.	Do you enjoy talking on the phone?	0	5	10
12.	How willing are you to work nights, scheduling subs?	0	5	10
13.	How easily are you intimidated by people?	0	5	10
14.	Do you have a shy personality?	0	5	10
15.	Can you make confident decisions?	0	5	10
16.	How much will you research remodeling principles?	0	5	10
17.	Are you sensitive to fumes and odors?	0	5	10
18.	Are you good with numbers?	0	5	10
19.	Do you have a creative mind?	0	5	10

ARE YOU READY TO BE YOUR OWN CONTRACTOR? (continued)

20. Can you visualize items from a
    written description?   o   5   10

21. Do you have strong self discipline?   o   5   10

22. Do you fluster easily?   o   5   10

23. Do problems cause you extreme stress?   o   5   10

24. Rate your organizational skills.   o   5   10

25. Are you vulnerable to sales pitches?   o   5   10

26. Do you have time to find subcontractors?   o   5   10

27. Do you enjoy negotiating for the best price? o   5   10

28. Is your checkbook balanced today?   o   5   10

29. Do you utilize a household budget?   o   5   10

30. Do you feel qualified to control irate
    subcontractors?   o   5   10

31. Do you have strong self confidence?   o   5   10

32. Do you lose your temper easily?   o   5   10

33. Can you react quickly to unexpected events? o   5   10

34. Can you make personal calls from work?   o   5   10

35. Do you buy bargains, even when you don't
    need the items?   o   5   10

36. Is your time financially valuable?   o   5   10

37. Will you be available to meet code
    enforcement inspectors?   o   5   10

38. Do you have a gambler's personality?   o   5   10

(continues)

ARE YOU READY TO BE YOUR OWN CONTRACTOR? (continued)

39.	Can you be assertive?	0	5	10
40.	Do you enjoy reading technical reports and articles?	0	5	10
41.	Do you retain information you read?	0	5	10
42.	Do you pay attention to small details?	0	5	10
43.	Do you know people who work in the trades?	0	5	10
44.	Do you trust your judgement?	0	5	10
45.	Can you keep accurate, written records?	0	5	10
46.	Are you able to do more than one task at a time?	0	5	10
47.	How well can you prioritize your day and your duties?	0	5	10
48.	Do you feel qualified to coordinate your project?	0	5	10
49.	Can you stand to watch your house being torn apart?	0	5	10
50.	Are you capable of staying out of the way of the workers?	0	5	10

Add your total score and compare it to the ranges given below to get an idea of your ability to act as the general contractor.

SCORES AND OPTIONS

If your score is 186 or less, seriously consider hiring a professional general contractor. Your answers indicate a weakness to perform the functions of a general contractor. This score may mean you do not have the right personality for the job. Technical points can be learned, but personalities are hard to change. You may be able to accomplish the task if you do extensive research and address your weak points. Keep your quiz answers in mind as you read this book. The book will help you to clearly identify the areas you need to address. For homeowners in this scoring range, hiring a professional is the safest route to take. Before trying to coordinate your own job, read this book and evaluate what you learn. Chances are, you will decide to hire a professional to manage your job. There is nothing wrong with this. Not all people are designed to run construction crews and jobs.

If your score is between 186 and 280, you have the ability to learn how to get the job done. Most of the areas you need to work on are remodeling related and can be learned. In this mid-range, you should be able to read enough to attempt the job at hand. Your score indicates some areas of weakness. As you complete this book, note the areas of weakness in your knowledge. Spend the time needed to strengthen these areas. With enough preliminary planning, you should be able to run your own job.

If you scored between 280 and 375, you are a natural. With the right research, you can be an excellent general contractor. The higher your score, the better qualified you are. If you scored near 375, all you will need to do is polish your knowledge of the trades; you already possess the basic qualities of a good general contractor. Even with a high score, you still have a lot to learn. Complete this book and, when you feel completely comfortable with your abilities, move ahead. You will be ready to command your construction crews and save money.

2

Hiring a
General Contractor

Selecting the right contractor is like culling crops. You must disregard the weak, the camouflaged, and the unreliable. The first step in weeding out bad contractors is to go to the telephone. Telephones are the arteries of strong remodeling and home- improvement firms. Communication is critical to a satisfying job. When you begin your search for contractors, you start with the telephone. Your phone will see a lot of use before and during the remodeling or improvement venture. There will be questions and concerns about the project. When they arise, you will need to be able to contact your contractor. The phone can tell you much about a contractor before you ever talk to the business owner.

Answering machines are disliked by almost everyone. When you take the time to call a company, you expect to get information right away, not after the beep. Recorded messages are offensive to many people. Others think it is rude to have a business phone answered electronically. If a machine answers your initial call to a contractor, what will your opinion be? Answering machines are used for many different reasons and do not necessarily indicate a bad or disreputable contractor. Maybe the contractor spends much of his or her time supervising or working on jobs. These are two qualities to look for in a good contractor. When the general is on the job, fewer problems occur.

A positive aspect of answering machines is that they keep overhead costs down. Receptionists and secretaries increase overhead significantly and may be unnecessary for small firms. As a customer you pay for increased overhead, which is passed on through higher prices. The contractor with an answering machine may be less expensive.

Some contractors use answering machines to screen calls. This is not a desirable trait. Contractors who screen their calls usually have dissatisfied customers or hounding creditors. There is a way to distinguish between the two purposes of an answering machine. Call early in the morning and again around 6:30 P.M. See if the contractor answers the phone. The contractor using a machine to keep costs low will probably be coordinating work at these times and should answer your call personally. The machine will answer the phone 24 hours a day, acting as a buffer for the undesirable contractor.

Regardless of their purpose, answering machines eliminate your ability to talk with the contractor immediately. Even if the contractor checks for messages regularly, you will not be able to reach the contractor right away. This can be a pivotal problem if something serious goes wrong on your job. All you can do is leave a recorded message, with no way of knowing when your call will be returned. This could be reason enough to disqualify the contractor from your consideration.

When you begin the search for contractors, keep a log. Enter the contractor's name, phone number, the date, and the time you called. When the contractor returns your call, note the time and date in the log. This may sound excessive or silly, but it can tell you a lot about a potential contractor.

You might be surprised by how many contractors will never return your call. It continually amazes me how contractors can

PHONE LOG			
Date	Company Name	Contact Person	Remarks

remain in business without returning phone calls. A successful contracting company depends on new business, and the refusal to return phone calls is business suicide. Some contractors will return the call but only after two or three days. The phone log helps you spot these red flags.

> Contractors should return your initial call within a few hours. If the contractor is working in the field, it may be evening before your call is reciprocated.

If it takes this long to speak with the contractor, there is a problem. Slow response to a request for new work means no response to calls about work done poorly. Contractors should return your initial call within a few hours. If the contractor is working in the field, it may be evening before your call is reciprocated. A good contractor will tend to present clients first and then potential customers. Although your message may receive lower priority, you should not have to wait days for a return call.

Phone response is an important element in choosing any contractor. If a contractor uses a receptionist or personal answering service, he or she can be reached quickly. The answering service should be capable of paging the contractor or calling him on the job site. Many contractors have a mobile phone or truck radio and will check in with the service periodically.

In today's competitive market, most successful contractors utilize cellular technology. Ask the answering service when your message will be conveyed to the contractor and how long it will be before you can expect a call. Write the information in the log, then wait and see if the time estimate was accurate. You shouldn't base a remodeling or home-improvement decision on the empty promise of a rapid response.

> There should also be a way for you the reach the contractor immediately in a crisis situation. An answering service can promptly relay your call for help; an answering machine cannot. A cell phone is even better.

Two hours' turnaround time is acceptable when you are not an existing customer. Once your job is started, your calls should be returned within an hour or less. There should also be a way for you the reach the contractor immediately in a crisis situation. An answering service can promptly relay your call for help; an answering machine cannot. A cell phone is even better. Overhead costs for the contractor remains low with an answering service, and the phones can be tended 24-hours a day. For the small contractor this is the sensible solution to the phone challenge. For the consumer it is an acceptable arrangement, combining fast phone responses with lower contract prices.

Contractors with administrative personnel and offices offer consumers a sense of security. The customer can go to an office and speak with the contractor or his office staff. Unless the contractor is doing a high volume of business, you will pay more for these conveniences. This secure, professional appearance can also be misleading. Offices and administrative assistants don't make good contractors.

> Do not be lulled into a false sense of security by outward appearances. It is possible that the office rent hasn't been paid for in months or the administrative staff is from a temporary service. The office furniture and equipment could be on a monthly lease. You can't judge contractors on appearance alone.

Finding the right contractor requires attention to detail and a well-conceived plan. A phone log is only the beginning, as it allows you to eliminate some contractors right away. If they don't perform well in your phone test, they won't perform well on your job. Delete contractors who don't promptly return your call; they obviously don't want or need your job. If they don't care enough to return your calls, forget them. You are looking for a good contractor with a desire to do your job. Ask them questions and record their answers on paper to keep in a file. Keep a list of the subcontractors with whom you may work.

Your Company Name
Your Company Address
Your Company Phone and Fax Numbers

SUBCONTRACTOR QUESTIONNAIRE

Company name: _____

Physical company address: _____

Company mailing address: _____

Company phone number: _____

After-hours phone number: _____

Company president/owner: _____

President/owner address: _____

President/owner phone number: _____

How long has company been in business? _____

Name of insurance company: _____

Insurance company phone number: _____

Does company have liability insurance? _____

Amount of liability insurance coverage: _____

Does company have worker's comp. insurance? _____

Type of work company is licensed to do: _____

List business or other license numbers: _____

Where are licenses held? _____

If applicable, are all workers licensed? _____

Are there any lawsuits pending against the company? _____

Has the company ever been sued? _____

Does the company use subcontractors? _____

Is the company bonded? _____

With whom is the company bonded? _____

Has the company had complaints filed against it? _____

Are there any judgments against the company? _____

SUBCONTRACTOR LIST

Service	Vendor	Phone	Date

The right contractor will understand your needs and strive to meet them. There are good contractors available, but finding them can be a challenge. Like any good result in life, locating the right contractor takes time. You will have to look hard to pinpoint exceptional contractors, and inducing them to do your job may take some creative maneuvering. These high-demand contractors have plenty of work. Don't despair; there are ways to attract the best contractors.

> Delete contractors who don't promptly return your call, as they obviously don't want or need your job. If they don't care enough to return your calls, forget them.

Where should you start your contractor quest? The Yellow Pages are a logical answer. Here you will find contractors who have been in business for awhile. It takes time to get into the book, and the advertising rates are steep. If you really want to do your homework, check the phone company for back issues of the Yellow Pages. You can chronicle a contractor's business history by noting the size and style of the ad over a period of time. The general contractors listed cover every aspect of construction and remodeling. Many of the ads will list the contractor's specialties. You must sift through the list to find suitable contractors for your job.

Advertisements in the classified section of your paper are another good resource for names. These contractors are probably either hungry or starting in business. Cross-check to see if the contractor is also listed in the phone book and Yellow Pages. Here is a quick tip on telephone advertising. If the contractor advertises in the paper as "John Doe Building," he should also be listed as "John Doe Building" in the phone book. If you find a listing in the white pages for "Mr. John Doe" and no Yellow Page listing, you can assume he operates from home without a business phone number. If you don't find "John Doe Building" in the line listings, he is probably a rookie or part-timer.

This isn't always bad. John Doe may have years of field experience with other contractors. This background can override the lack of business experience, and you might get your best deal from John Doe. If Mr. Doe tells you he has ten employees and has been in business for fifteen years, be cautious. The phone company is not in the habit of allowing people to operate a business from their home without paying additional fees. Official businesses are customarily given a free line listing in the phone book. A little research can go a long way in testing the validity of a contractor.

Another effective way to find contractors is by doing some undercover work around your neighborhood. Look for jobs in progress on other houses. When you see a contractor's sign or truck, write down the name and phone number. Jot down the address of the house where the work is being done. These jobs can be future references to check for potential contractors.

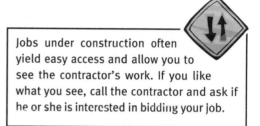

Jobs under construction often yield easy access and allow you to see the contractor's work. If you like what you see, call the contractor and ask if he or she is interested in bidding your job.

Explain that your house is close to the one the contractor is working on; ask to walk through the job in progress with the contractor. Finished jobs are much more difficult to gain access to because homeowners don't appreciate a parade of people going through their recently renovated house. During the remodeling process, homeowners expect a lot of traffic. Take advantage of your timing, and go see the work while you can. If you get the opportunity, ask the homeowners if they are satisfied with the contractor and the work.

Do you know anyone who recently had renovation work done? Friends and acquaintances are a reliable resource, because you get the names of tradespeople who have done satisfactory work for people you know personally. Do not take this information as the absolute solution to your contractor search. Before running out and signing a contract, ask yourself a few questions. Was the work done for your friends similar to the work you want done? If they had their bathroom remodeled, it doesn't automatically qualify the contractor to build your dormer addition. A contractor capable of building exquisite decks isn't always the best candidate for extensive kitchen remodeling.

Networking among reputable contractors increases the chances of finding a good contractor for your job.

Make sure the contractor is qualified to complete the work you want done. If not, consider contacting the contractor and asking for references of other tradespeople in your specific area. Good contractors do not associate with unprofessional, amateurs who might tarnish their reputations. Networking among reputable contractors increases the chances of finding a good contractor for your job. Mentioning that you were referred by a fellow contractor or satisfied customer also carries a lot of weight.

The first step in finding the right contractor is establishing your needs. Make an outline of the type of work you want done. Do you plan to build a garage? A competent contractor in bath and kitchen remodeling may not be the best choice to construct your garage. The bath contractor works with existing interior conditions, as opposed to footings, site work, or rafters. Check out your contractors carefully and compare their qualifications to your specifications.

Many remodelers are specialists in their field. Remodeling has become increasingly complex and can be compared to medical services. Would you go to a pediatrician for advice on a heart condition? A dormer addition requires a specialist, experienced in cutting open a roof and the many structural changes involved. The knowledge required for work of this magnitude is different from the experience needed to finish a basement. The company that did a great job on your neighbor's basement could prove to be a disaster for your dormer addition. Whenever possible, you want to compare apples to apples and to differentiate the knowledge and skill needed for the job at hand.

There is almost no comparison between building a dormer and finishing a basement. Basement work doesn't usually

OUTLINE OF WORK TO BE DONE

GARAGE CONSTRUCTION

Choose style of garage desired.

Draw a rough draft of garage or obtain a pre-drawn plan.

Make or obtain a list of required materials.

Select materials to be used.

Price materials.

Make list of contractors needed or a list of general contractors.

Contact contractors.

Obtain labor quotes.

Evaluate budget needs and ability to afford the garage.

Make financing arrangements.

Make final decision on plan to be built.

Choose contractors and check references.

Meet with attorney to draw-up contracts and other documents.

Make commitments to suppliers and contractors.

Schedule work.

Start work.

Inspect work.

Obtain copies of code enforcement inspections.

Make required payments and have lien waivers signed.

Inspect completed job.

Make punch-list, if necessary.

Make absolute final inspection and approval.

Make final payments, except for retainages.

Make retainage payments.

(continues)

OUTLINE OF WORK TO BE DONE (continued

CATEGORIES OF WORK TO BE DONE

Survey	Framing	Painting
Blueprints	Windows	Electrical work
Permits	Doors	Insulation
Site work	Sheathing	Drywall
Footing	Roofing	Electric door
Foundation	Siding	openers
Floor preparation	Trim work	Landscaping
Floor		

require any structural expertise. A contractor doesn't have to contend with inclement weather or rafter cuts. Finishing a basement has its own challenges with support columns and altering existing conditions. Proper care to control moisture is another skill necessary in finishing a basement. With a dormer contractors have to know how to deal with rain, wind, and snow. Most of the work is new construction, and existing conditions only play a small role. The contractors who execute these jobs can be as different as the two types of work performed. A comparison will show both types of contractors are professionals in their field.

There may be a few contractors capable of doing both types of work well, but this is the exception rather than the rule. Finding a well-rounded, fully experienced contractor is rare. The majority of contractors specialize in closely defined areas of remodeling, which are determined by several factors. Some contractors concentrate on the jobs offering the highest profit, and others specialize in work they enjoy. You must determine a potential contractor's weaknesses and strengths. Usually the work a contractor does most often is the work he or she does the best.

The fields of specialization can cover any aspect of remodeling and improvements. Some examples include:

- Garages can be a specialty.
- Sunrooms are a common specialty.
- Dormers can be a specialty.
- Additions offer the opportunity for specialization.
- Kitchens are a natural specialty.
- Bathrooms are one of the most popular rooms in a home to remodel.

Some companies stress their special talents through advertising. The bulk of newspaper ads consist of newer businesses. Many haven't been established long enough to get in the Yellow Pages. Newspaper ads and fliers are easy sources of effective advertising for young businesses.

> Contractors just starting out can be an inexpensive alternative to get your job done. With the right precautions, new businesses can result in exceptional values.

New businesses need your work and will try very hard to win your job. Your negotiating power is stronger with these contractors. While they are new in business, they may be extremely good at what they do. They may have years of experience working for another company, and experience is what you are looking for. It doesn't matter where they learned to do the job as long as they do it right. The contractor who sits behind a desk for five years could have less experience than the tradesperson just starting a

> There is some risk to a new company, since it is more likely to fail. This will result in trouble when a warranty problem arises. You could get well into the remodeling process, only to have the company close its doors. Getting another contractor to come in to finish someone else's work isn't easy, and it will be expensive. To reduce this problem, stay in control. Be prepared for the worst and never let the contractors have more money than has been earned.

business. Your interest is in their remodeling experience, not their business degree.

Rules of the Road

- Do not be afraid to use a new company; the savings often offset the risks.
- Maintain control.
- Don't give the contractor a large cash deposit.
- Put everything in writing.
- Inspect all work closely before advancing any money.
- Insist on lien waivers when any money is paid.
- Ask for original certificates of insurance before any work is started; these should be provided to you without delay from the insurance company.
- Ask for three credit references.
- Obtain several job references.
- Follow up on the references and ask to see actual examples of the contractor's work. It's easy to give friends and relatives as job references, so check them out personally.
- Request evidence of the contractor's state and local license numbers.
- Ask for the contractor's address; this will make a bad apple squirm.
- Validate and investigate all the information to protect yourself against the unforeseen.

These basic rules should be used with any contractor. A company in business for ten years can be out of business in a day. The longer a company has been in business, the more time they've had to get into financial trouble. Businesses that grow too fast sink even faster. From the outside, a company can look extremely successful even when it is in deep trouble.

Shiny new trucks, fancy offices, and large management staffs are impressive but expensive. A company with these expenses must compensate for its overhead with volume or higher prices. Any company with extensive overhead is a potential bankruptcy case. And this can be bad for you.

A contractor may have been successful for the last several years and still get in trouble fast. A growing business, with heavy overhead can be derailed by a slow economy. If the company's

> You can be hurt by either an established company or a new one. You have to protect yourself at all times.

volume of business declines, it can't afford its overhead. Items such as a fleet of trucks and expensive offices quickly consume any reserve capital. When this happens, a once successful company fails. Don't be fooled by an impressive exterior appearance. Keep your guard up, and make all contractors play by the rules.

If you find a contractor from newspaper or Yellow Pages ads, be selective. Call enough contractors to get a fair assessment of the talent available. Evaluate each contractor. Ask questions, get everything in writing, and don't assume anything. It is important to establish a position of control from the beginning. Reputable contractors will respect you for

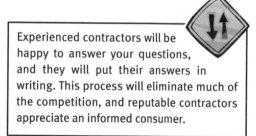

Experienced contractors will be happy to answer your questions, and they will put their answers in writing. This process will eliminate much of the competition, and reputable contractors appreciate an informed consumer.

your knowledgeable business practices. If you know enough to ask the right questions, the quality contractor will get your job. They don't have to worry about the fast-talking, hard-selling, low bidder. When you are ready to schedule your subcontractors, make a written record of the schedule.

Good contractors constantly fight the price-war battle with questionable contractors. They have to survive without using the

SUBCONTRACTOR SCHEDULE

Type of Service	Vendor Name	Phone Number	Date Scheduled

Notes/Changes:

slick tactics of less honorable companies. Regardless of the game, playing by the rules is the hardest way to win. In the remodeling arena there are a lot of people looking to win at the customer's expense. The best contractors are in business for the long haul, and your satisfaction will mean more business down the road. They know you will call again for future work or refer them to your friends. Word-of-mouth advertising is the best a contractor can have. It is inexpensive and produces a consistent flow of good work.

Contractors living on the dark side will not have these concerns. They are looking to make a fast buck. They aren't building a business. They're making money. Their objective is to get your money, and they operate on a one-shot basis. In larger cities they survive because of the turnover of residents. In many urban areas a contractor can get to you before his reputation does.

Large cities are a perfect breeding ground for shoddy work. The environment allows renegade contractors to run rampant. They know their present customers aren't likely to affect future business. All these contractors concentrate on getting jobs so they can get the customer's money. Many contractors have refined this approach into an art. They utilize good advertising and trained salespeople to thrive in the city. They know all the ways to stay one step ahead of you. Unfortunately, their methods are legal, and their tactics are well defined.

They prey on uninformed homeowners. With demographic studies they can attack the market of their choice. These are not contractors. They are professional sales forces. When selling to first-time homeowners, they may arrive in a compact car so as not to appear overly successful. The objective is to appear on the same financial level as the consumer.

When working a different neighborhood, the vehicle of choice may be a four-wheel-drive pickup truck. This is the "Good Ole Boy" approach, designed to assure you that the contractor works just as hard as you do for his money. Such salespeople will wear jeans and flannel shirts, with boots and a tape measure. They will take notes on a metal clipboard to give the illusion of a working contractor. Some people respond better to a general contractor who works on the job himself. These camouflaged salespeople prey on a homeowner's weaknesses. They know how to do it and make their living selling jobs. I have seen these people in action. They often sell more jobs than the workers can complete. It's up to the scheduling department to juggle irate homeowners like hot potatoes.

In upper-class neighborhoods, these birds of prey arrive in a luxury car: wearing a three-piece suit and carrying a leather briefcase. Laptop computers and gold pens will be part of their arsenal of sales tools. This is the "Dress For Success" method, giving the contractor the image of a dynamic, prosperous businessperson. He acknowledges that your time is valuable and points out that his is, too. He suggests that he can squeeze you into his busy schedule if you sign the contract tonight.

Use common sense, and never allow yourself to be pressured or persuaded into a commitment.

Is this the kind of game you want to play? It shouldn't be, unless you are willing to lose. These sales-oriented professionals seldom have any field experience in remodeling. It is likely that they use subcontractors for all the work. Their prices will be inflated to allow a hefty profit for their time; you are probably paying them a commission to sell you the job. Why should you keep them in expensive suits and luxury cars? Cut them out and enjoy the money yourself; you probably know as much about remodeling as they do.

A call to the Better Business Bureau or Contractor Licensing Board can tell you if the contractor has been reported for adverse or illegal business practices.

Calling a contractor you know nothing about is risky. A business card picked up from the community bulletin board could produce a good deal or a remodeling rip-off artist. Advertisements in free newspapers deserve a phone call, but be wary. There are unlimited ways to find good contractors. The tricky part is finding a suitable contractor for the type of work you want done. Not all contractors are created equal. Some are better than others in specialized areas.

Don't sign anything without thinking and without reviewing the documents. Ask about material and work guarantees, and be sure to get them in writing. Requiring the contractor to use your contract will immediately weed through many of the sharks. Remove their fancy clauses and legal rhetoric and you pull their teeth. Swing the pendulum in your favor in every way possible. Read books and research your project before dealing with any contractors. Try to get a referral if at all possible. Do your homework before having work done on your home.

3

Plans and Specifications

PLANS

Turning your design ideas into reality requires working plans and specifications. Depending on the project, the plans can be simple line drawings or formal architectural plans. When you deal with a general contractor, he will supply the plans for you. Some general contractors draft
their own plans; many have the plans drawn by other professionals.
Remodeling demands a different approach from building a new house.
With new construction you might find suitable designs and specifications
in a plans book. These books offer numerous house plans at reasonable
rates. Unfortunately, it is difficult to mass-produce remodeling plans. No
two jobs are the same, and no one can anticipate the existing conditions
of your home. You will need to have custom plans drawn for your
remodeling project.

General contractors can help you finalize the design of your project. Experienced contractors can provide excellent advice and are
skilled in the execution of blueprints. They can show you the benefits

and drawbacks of your design ideas and answer your questions. While general contractors are not architects, they have much to offer in terms of blueprint preparation. They are the people in the field with the hands-on experience. If you are contemplating a design on paper, the contractor may have already built something similar. Hands-on experience of building and remodeling is invaluable in designing blueprints.

General contractors know first-hand what works and what only looks good on paper. Most have been in the business for some time and can give you several design ideas. Contractors will have their own designs and layouts that they have built for other people. They can tell you which designs cause trouble down the road. Bow windows are attractive but can cause water leaks where they attach to the house. If the window's roof is not properly flashed, your wall will rot away. Poor attic ventilation can result in structural damage. Attic ventilation is frequently overlooked by homeowners when they design an addition.

If your bedroom addition includes a cantilever, you will have a cold spot in the room. The area protruding over the foundation will be much colder than the rest of the room. Do you know how to reduce the effect of this cold spot? The contractor will know the techniques that work best. His or her knowledge will also be invaluable in preparing the specifications for your project. Where should the plumbing for your kitchen sink be roughed in? If you put the water pipes in the outside wall, you could be in for an unpleasant surprise in the winter. In cold climates, plumbing should not be placed in exterior walls, since pipes will freeze quickly on cold, windy

The local lumberyard is a good place to start when you are establishing a set of plans and specifications.

days. The pipes will freeze and rupture; as soon as the ice thaws, the broken pipe will flood your home. This can ruin your day as well as your kitchen. Experienced contractors will specify that the pipes come through the floor or into the side of the cabinets from an interior partition. There are a lot of advantages to working with contractors.

Running the show yourself requires that you do it all. The local lumberyard is a good place to start when you are establishing a set of plans and specifications. Review your material quotes on lumber prices, and take your rough draft to the lumberyard with the best price. Ask the manager if the company provides design services for their customers. Most large suppliers will be equipped to draw your plans, but they may ask for a commitment to buy the materials from them. If they are the low bidder on the job, this should not be a problem.

Ask them to guarantee their material prices until the job is complete. If they are willing to do this, make your commitment to buy there. The supplier will be reluctant to guarantee prices if the job will be in progress for a long time or will not start for quite awhile. Under these conditions, negotiate for a prearranged cost increase cap. This price cap protects you from runaway price increases while allowing you to get your plans now. Get your material quote in writing and have it signed by the manager to help you when doing cost projections.

> Material suppliers are reluctant to guarantee prices if a job will be in progress for a long time or will not start reasonably soon. Under these conditions, negotiate for a pre-arranged cost increase cap. This price cap protects you from runaway price increases.

Now you have locked in material prices and free plans. Think of all the money you saved in the cost of obtaining working plans. You may be wondering where the hook is in this deal. This is just too good to be true. Is there something wrong with the plans supplied by lumberyards? How do architects survive if suppliers will give you free plans? The hook is in the material sales. They provide the free plans to get your business. This is a practical option if they are the low bidder, because you don't lose anything. You gain a big savings in the

COST PROJECTIONS

Item/Phase	Labor	Material	Total
Total estimated expense			

cost of the plans preparation. There are some differences in the quality of the plans. Architectural plans are much more detailed and provide extensive specifications.

The plans and specifications you receive from a building supplier will be adequate for most jobs. They will be drawn to show the basics, and a qualified contractor will not have trouble working with these types of plans. The specifications will detail materials to be used but will not be as comprehensive as architectural plans. Some contractors react in a negative way to architectural plans and specifications, especially on an elementary project. They are frustrated by hundreds of pages of specifications. For these jobs, free plans certainly offer some advantages.

Code-enforcement offices will probably accept your line drawing for non-structural changes. If you are relocating walls or building an addition, they will want structural plans to work with. Your building-supply plans should be acceptable to your code-enforcement office, because they will show all the important structural features. These plans may not have as many elevations, detailed enlargements, or technical descriptions as architectural drawings, but they will be working plans. Do you need a detailed material legend on the plans? No, because this can be addressed in the contract and specifications sheet. You do not need it on the blueprints.

Points to Consider About Blueprints for Home Improvements

- Blueprints are a reference point in remodeling.

- It is unlikely that the job will be completed exactly as shown on the plans.

- There will be unforeseen obstacles and personal changes that will deviate from the original plans.

- Why pay thousands of dollars for extensive plans, only to change them on the job?

- Remodeling is in a class by itself; there is nothing like it.

- Even the best plans are never good enough when dealing with unknown factors.
- Unknown factors result in on-the-job decisions and modifications.
- You can't plan on a definite outcome with remodeling.
- You will need working plans, but be prepared to make on-site changes as well.

Your preliminary design might be all you need. For some jobs, all you have to do is point an experienced remodeler in the right direction. Professional blueprints are not always a prerequisite to a good job. Established remodelers are specialists, with years of experience. They have dealt with adjustments throughout their career. A clear line drawing may be all the subcontractors need. Before spending money on commercial drawings, talk with the people who will be doing the work. They may be able to visualize the job and do their take-offs (material lists) without formal plans.

If your plans don't come from a building supplier, you still have options. Drafting companies are a possible alternative. Drafting firms will be happy to develop your design into blueprints. Find a company specializing in construction plans by looking through the phone book or contractor referrals. All of your experienced subcontractors will be accustomed to working from blueprints. Question them about companies that provide blueprinting services. As subcontractors, they don't have plans drawn, but they do work from them. They should be able to give you names of firms that supply working prints.

Your code officer is another source of referrals for blueprints. Code officers review plans on a daily basis. Ask them for names of companies to contact. They won't be able to recommend a specific drafting firm, but they can give you a list of places to investigate.

Take your rough draft with you when you interview various drafting companies. Show them your drawing and ask for a quote to convert your sketch into a set of working plans. For anywhere from a few hundred to a few thousand dollars, you might be able to get detailed plans and specifications that are suitable for small jobs. They won't be as extensive as an architectural package, but they will be adequate and much less expensive.

All the necessary structural information will be provided by a drafting firm. You can specify items such as bath fixtures, paint color, and other similar items in your contract or a separate specifications sheet. The plans produced by drafters will include more information than those from the building supplier but less than those from an architect. They are a happy medium. You will have the basic building plan and other diagrams. These will include electrical, plumbing, and heating diagrams. In addition, there will be front, back, and side elevations. You will get cross-section details and any pertinent information required by the code-enforcement office. For extensive or complex remodeling jobs, drafted plans will normally be better than those available through material suppliers.

Drafting-company plans consist mainly of blueprints. There will not be extensive specifications to accompany them. The information on the plans will detail the basic aspects of your

> The primary difference between drafted plans and architectural plans is the detailed specifications.

project. This includes size of structural members, the type of shingles to be used, siding, and other related areas. There will be details of your foundation and recommendations for the footings and concrete. You can expect to see all minimum code requirements on the plans. This is an efficient, economical way to get your project off the ground.

Architects are the most commonly thought of source for blueprint development. Architects are known for their ability to design outstanding projects. Another trademark of architects is their extensive

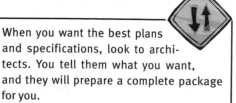

> When you want the best plans and specifications, look to architects. You tell them what you want, and they will prepare a complete package for you.

specification packages. Consider an architect for any work requiring an engineer, such as altering existing foundations, digging out and expanding buried basements, or raising your roof. Their services are expensive, but you get engineered plans and specs of the highest quality.

On large residential jobs and complicated projects, architects are very effective. They are responsible for the success or failure of large projects. Projects of this magnitude require architects, and you cannot afford to settle for anything less. Small remodeling jobs can benefit from the architect's abilities but can rarely support the expense. Intricate residential jobs may require their expertise. Evaluate your needs and determine which source of plans is the most logical for your job.

> If you want something truly unique, architects can provide it. If you want something special, they are the professionals to call.

If you rule out architectural drawings due to the expense, consider retaining an architect as a consultant. You derive the benefit of his or her training without paying for a complete architectural package. Having an architect available will make you more confident. He can answer your questions, and you are assured of unbiased answers. This advantage gives you an element of control over the contractors and provides you with knowledge you might not otherwise have.

Regardless of who draws your plans, they are done with pen and paper. Or in today's world, with computerized drawing software. The combination of skilled drawing techniques, experience, proper tools, and a creative mind will produce the best job. The strongest advice is to get good plans and great contractors. Your job can only be as good as the people doing the work. With a poor contractor, the best plans are only a piece of paper. Even if you act as the general contractor, you will be relying on your subcontractors. The success of any job revolves around organization and experienced tradespeople.

SPECIFICATIONS

The next requirement to discuss is specifications. These are the details that ensure that you get exactly what you want. When you buy a new car, you have the advantage of going for a test drive. You can see all the bells and whistles before you invest your money. With remodeling, you have to spell out every detail from the number and type of doors to the paint colors. When you deal with contractors and suppliers, they will make recommendations. Examine their recommendations carefully. Don't be coerced into expensive products you don't need or talked out of custom changes you want. Throughout the project, you will have to be cautious of camouflaged sales-people. Homeowners don't usually identify architects, contractors, and building-supply managers as salespeople, but sales techniques allow them to increase their profit.

Before entering into a contract or finalizing your plans, know what you want. Be sure of what it will cost, and make sure it has been properly specified.

Be open to suggestions, but don't blindly accept recommendations that increase your cost. I have seen jobs start at $3,000 and wind up costing more than $9,000. If the additional expenses and upgrades are your idea, that's fine. Make sure they are not a decision made under pressure or out of ignorance. Regardless of the conclusion you draw, be certain to include thorough information in your specification.

The most effective way to avoid cost overruns is to specify the job yourself. You may find that you are not qualified to coordinate the remodeling process, but you know what you want. Why pay someone to tell you what you already know? The blueprints will specify the areas beyond your knowledge. You can easily detail your desired fixtures and finishes yourself.

Your specifications should be laid out in chronological order. You simply express what you want in writing, and make it a part of all contracts. The spec sheet can be simple

When your specifications are complete, make several copies. Have the contractors initial each page and sign the last page. Refer to the specifications in your contract. This will protect you during the job. With the contractor's initials and signature on the specifications, they can't claim a misunderstanding.

Specifications should be, as the name implies, specific. Do not leave anything to the imagination. Define brands, model numbers, manufacturers, colors, and any other descriptive language. Do not allow substitutions without your written consent.

or complex. It depends on the type of job you are doing. The more details you include, the less problems you will have later. You must not forget anything. When contractors bid based on plans and specs, that is what you get. If you have omitted something in the specifications, you will have to pay extra for it later.

The following is an example of the correct way to prepare your specifications:

Rough-In Plumbing Specifications

The plumbing contractor shall adhere to the following specifications:

1. The plumbing contractor shall supply all required licenses and permits to complete the following work. All work will be done in compliance with state and local plumbing codes.

2. All plumbing will be installed as detailed by the plans and specifications for the job labeled "John Doe, 123 Pleasant St, Happyville, U.S."

3. No substitutions shall be made without written consent of the property owner.

4. All water distribution pipe shall be type "L," rigid copper tubing.

5. All drain, waste, and vent piping and fittings shall be schedule 40, PVC.

6. Tub and shower faucets shall be single-handle, chrome finish, with pressure- balance control. They shall be manufactured by the "Drip-Be-Gone" company, model #1672.

7. Shower-head arm outlets shall be located 6' 6" from the finished floor level.

8. Toilets shall be 12" rough, round front, 1.6 gallon, water savers, manufactured by "Throne," in designer Sand color #THS-02, model #9001. Toilets shall be supplied with matching plastic seats from the "Throne" company, model #8001.

9. Drop-in lavatories shall be manufactured by "Dinky Sink," in Sand color #S65, model #47.

10. Lavatory faucets shall be "Drip-Be-Gone," single-handle, model #2579, with a chrome finish.

11. The kitchen sink shall be a "Tin Man," stainless-steel, five-hole, double-bowl sink, model #345.

12. The kitchen faucet shall be a "Wash-A-Lot" single handle, model #0089, with spray attachment, in a chrome finish.

13. The dishwasher, supplied by owner, will be connected by the plumbing contractor. The plumbing contractor will supply an air gap, copper hot water line, with valve, and all drain hoses and connectors.

14. The owner-supplied icemaker shall be connected by the plumbing contractor. The plumbing contractor shall make this connection and provide a valve and copper tubing.

15. The new washing-machine location will be provided with a metal washer outlet box. This receptacle will be supplied and installed by the plumbing contractor.

16. All vent pipes penetrating the roof will be flashed and sealed against leakage by the plumbing contractor.

17. The plumbing contractor will be responsible for the cleanup, on a daily basis, of all areas disturbed by plumbing-related work.

18. The plumbing contractor will agree to and sign a subcontractor agreement before any work is commenced.

19. Any changes in these specifications will only be recognized if agreed to in writing by the property owner.

With detailed specifications and thorough contracts, you will eliminate many of the problems associated with remodeling. If you stand by your plans and specifications, you remove the threat of skilled salespeople. They will only be able to sell you what is on the plans and specs. Their attempts to upgrade your material choices will have no effect. If you don't maintain this self-control, you can ultimately buy much more than you expected.

It is very easy to get caught up in the excitement of your remodeling project. Your judgment can be overrun with desire. When this happens, you lose control. Don't let this happen.

After talking to a skilled salesperson, your perspective can change. The exterior doors you loved yesterday can't compare with the ones offered by the salesperson. They will divert your attention and confuse you. Once you are not sure of your choice, selling their product is much easier. This is the beginning of an expensive lesson. The salespeople will capitalize on your indecision.

Think before you act. Don't deviate from your original plans without serious consideration.

With their skills they will coerce you into buying their products. This type of impulse buying will destroy your budget.

If the supplier doesn't have access to the brands you specified, he or she will try to sell you the store brand. They will have supporting documentation to verify the quality of their product.

Their product could be as good as or better than the one you specified, but you spent extensive time researching your chosen products. Are you willing to throw that time and information away for a quick decision? Think before you act. Don't deviate from your original plans without serious consideration.

Contractors can be very effective salespeople, too. Once they have your confidence, you are an easy target. They may point out ways to improve on your plans. These improvements can come at a high price. They know, once they have the job, that you are not likely to shop for prices on extras and changes. If they can convince you to change your plans, they can increase their profit. Some contractors specialize in upgrading customers. They come in low and leave high. These guys are dangerous to your budget.

A contractor armed with good sales techniques can sell you almost anything. If the contractor who is working on the job brings a problem to your attention, will you seek a second opinion? A common reaction is immediately to authorize the contractor to rectify the situation. Most contractors will treat you fairly, but some won't. The bad guys know how to take advantage of you. They get well into the job before approaching you on changes or extras. By this time you have come to trust them. If they tell you that your house needs additional work, you will probably believe them. They will stress the savings of having the work done now while they are already on the job. This is a standard sales pitch given to homeowners.

Often a subcontractor who is responsible for supplying material or fixtures will tell you the product is unavailable. Then he will offer you substitutions, which are either upgrades or items designed to make price comparisons impossible. Call

> Should you get other estimates before authorizing the contractor to do the work? Get at least one other opinion. Having at least three quotes is better. There are contractors that make their living by taking advantage of trusting consumers.

Your Company Name
Your Company Address
Your Company Phone and Fax Numbers

REQUEST FOR SUBSTITUTIONS

Customer name: _____

Customer address: _____

Customer city/state/zip: _____

Customer phone number: _____

Job location: _____

Plans and specifications dated: _____

Bid requested from: _____

Type of work: _____

The following items are being substituted for the items specified in the attached plans and specifications: _____

_____

_____

_____

_____

_____

Please indicate your acceptance of these substitutions by signing below.

_____		_____	
Contractor	Date	Customer	Date
		_____	
		Customer	Date

his hand and corroborate his statements. Ask the name of the suppliers he gets his materials from and which of them he has checked stock with. It may be that the item is only temporarily out of stock or can be obtained through another supplier. Subcontractors may not receive the same discount from each supplier; therefore, they may not investigate all the available options. If the contractor truly cannot acquire the item through his sources, consider omitting it from his contract price. Offer to supply the product yourself. Faced with the prospect of losing his mark-up on the item, the subcontractor may miraculously find the product in stock somewhere.

Don't take anything for granted; protect yourself at all times. If the cost of unforeseen work is only $100, it probably isn't worth the time spent in getting other estimates. If contractors tell you they can't get an item, check the availability yourself. Use your own judgment, but beware of substitutions and extras. Maintain control with your established plans and specifications.

You can create a specification sheet. The products you have in mind will give you the information to include for the major items. For more technical information, you may need to visit the library or go online. There are several home-improvement reference books available. These books will help you detail lesser-known specifics. Using the Internet is an excellent way to shop for specifications from home. These specifications tie the hands of crooked contractors. They cannot beat you when they have to play by your rules. As a consumer or a general contractor, it's important for you to maintain control.

One of the best ways to control your job is with detailed, written instruments.

Many factors give you the control needed for a successful job. One is detailed plans and specifications. Spend the time to do them right. Do not cut corners on the specifications. Don't assume the subcontractors or suppliers know what you want. Don't consider an aspect discussed and understood unless you have specified it in writing.

The time you spend now will save you frustration later. Keep the specifications clear and concise. Don't give contractors and suppliers a gap to slip through. Refer to your plans throughout the contract and specifications. If necessary, label certain areas to clarify your descriptions.

4

Putting Your Job
Out for Bids

R emodeling like any construction project, requires people to perform the work and supply the materials to work with. These two factors account for most of the costs incurred in a remodeling project. To stay on budget, you have to control both of these expenses. The most effective way to control job costs is with written quotes. Your goal is to expedite accurate quote, and compare the information to establish the best value for your investment dollar. Collecting quotes allows you to establish conclusive budget figures and finalize your plans and specifications. This is not a complicated process, but it requires an eye for details.

Most aspects of cost estimating deal primarily with product selection and costs for tubs, cabinets, flooring, and so on that you have selected. To calculate the project's total costs, both hard and soft costs must be included. Hard costs consist of footings, foundations, carpentry, plumbing, electrical labor, and other mandatory construction phases. Soft costs include such items as insurance premiums.

It is easy to overlook the smaller aspects of a remodeling job. These oversights can be expensive. Trash removal, permit fees, and cleanup costs are good examples of frequently missed expenditures. By using a cost-estimate form, you will see these classifications and know if you need to include an item in your quotes. The categories will provide you with the information necessary to test the integrity of labor and material quotes. For example, does the contractor's quote include rip-out, cleanup, and removal of all debris? It should be spelled out clearly in the quote.

> Soliciting bids for labor and materials is a very important step in starting a project. The success of your job hinges on solid quotes.

ESTIMATES

When remodeling costs get out of hand, often due to faulty estimates, the job suffers, and corners must be cut to save money. Careful planning eliminates compromises and allows your dreams to become reality. Estimates give you a monetary range to work within, but quotes are needed in the final budgeting phase. Don't confuse an estimate with a quote.

Prices listed in an estimate can fluctuate greatly, and some contractors use low estimates as a sales tactic. They plan to get into a job by being the low bidder and then add to their price with extras. Work you thought was included in the original price suddenly becomes an additional expense. This procedure allows a contractor to be the low bidder initially and ultimately leave your job with more money than the competitors.

> The difference between an estimate and a quote can mean thousands of dollars to you. Estimates are like a hypothesis; they are educated guesses.

How can they get away with this? The estimate is their escape path. Estimates only include a vague description of the work to be done, leaving much room for interpretation and problems. I once took my truck in to be serviced. I was careful to ask for an estimate of the repair

Your Company Name
Your Company Address
Your Company Phone and Fax Numbers

WORK ESTIMATE

Date: _____

Customer name: _____

Customer address: _____

Customer phone number(s): _____

DESCRIPTION OF WORK

Your Company Name will supply all labor and material for the following work:

_____

_____

_____

PAYMENT FOR WORK

Estimated price: _____ ($ _____)

Payable as follows: _____

_____

If you have any questions, please don't hesitate to call. Upon acceptance, a formal contract will be issued.
Respectfully submitted,

Your Name _____

Title _____

Your Company Name
Your Company Address
Your Company Phone and Fax Numbers

QUOTE

This agreement, made this _____ day of _____,
20__, shall set forth the whole agreement, in its entirety, by and between
Your Company Name, herein called Contractor, and _____,
herein called Owners.

Job name: _____

Job location: _____

The Contractor and Owners agree to the following: Contractor shall
perform all work as described below and provide all material to complete
the work described below. Contractor shall supply all labor and material to
complete the work according to the attached plans and specifications.The
work shall include the following:

_____
_____
_____

SCHEDULE

The work described above shall begin within _____ days of notice from
Owners, with an estimated start date of _____. The
Contractor shall complete the above work in a professional and expedient
manner within _____ days from the start date.

PAYMENT SCHEDULE

Payment shall be made as follows: _____
_____

This agreement, entered into on _____, shall
constitute the whole agreement between Contractor and Owners.

_____   _____
Contractor   Date   Owner   Date

                                     _____
                                      Owner   Date

cost, and it seemed like a reasonable price. The final bill included additional parts, extra labor, and freight charges! "The first price was only an estimate," replied the manager, "Once we got into it, we found more problems." It is risky to allow anyone to work with only an estimated cost projection.

Estimates may contain a lot of words, but they might not mean much. How do they compare with quotes? There are many differences. The estimate only contains a few specific details, such as: the room to be painted, color of the paint, and how the paint will be applied. Detail will be reserved for the payment schedule, which will be very clear and require a deposit upon acceptance of the estimate. The next payment could be due when the material is delivered to the job, with the final payment due upon completion.

Does this appear to be an acceptable estimate? After all, the location, color, and type of paint have all been clearly specified. What other considerations exist in a painting proposal? Visualizing the painting process will allow you to discover the omissions. Interior painting will involve moving furniture. Whose responsibility is it? Will protection from spillage be provided by you or the contractor? You can bet an estimate will not address these matters.

Does the estimate say how long the job will take? Will primer or sealant be used before the paint is applied? Most estimates will not answer these questions. What hours of the day will the work be done? Maybe the contractor has a full-time job and only paints in the evening. When an estimate says the contractor will paint the walls and ceiling of your family room, what is actually included? Are they going to paint the baseboards and window and door trim as well? Are the holes and dings in the wall going to be patched before the walls are painted?

Another unanswered question involves the type of paint. Will it be flat or semi-gloss? The contractor agreed orally to allow your choice of paint, but paint prices vary with quality and type. What will you do when the contractor charges extra for the paint you selected? What happens if he or she tells you after the fact that the price was for a builder-grade paint, and your selection was a more expensive custom color? Do you have to pay the additional cost? The contractor will say yes and you will say no, but ultimately it may be up to a to judge decide. The bottom line is that an estimate cannot be compared to or considered to be a quote. You will have a difficult time suing someone for a guess, but a quote is an absolute commitment.

Even though contracts are more specific than quotes, not all contracts are created equal. Make sure that the quote addresses all the pertinent concerns. A proposal may, for example, says that the contractor will supply plastic for the floors, but whose responsibility is it to put it down? There is also no mention of protecting lights, outlet covers, and doors from overspray. The contractor may assure you that he will take care of this, but his contract specifically voids any verbal commitments. Empty promises can't be proved in court.

When you receive a quote, it is necessary to analyze the information and look for discrepancies. What may first appear to be a reasonable quote may turn out to be a nebulous, one-sided proposal.

Some homeowners are influenced by a contractor's low hourly labor rate and accept a proposal to do the project on a time and material basis. Whenever possible, avoid time-and-material agreements.

The description of the work states the walls, ceilings, and trim will be sprayed to allow proper coverage. How many coats are required, and what is proper coverage? Similar language mentions timely completion in a workmanlike manner. Who is to say what is timely or workmanlike?

TIME-AND-MATERIAL WORK

Costs can skyrocket during the process of a home improvement when a time-and-material work policy is in play. You have no control over the final cost of the work if you don't

SAMPLE PROPOSAL

PRESTO PAINT
170 SHADY PLACE
NOGO, OH 65478
(101) 555-2341

DATE: _June 12, 2004_
CUSTOMER NAME: _Mr. & Mrs. J. P. Homeowner_
ADDRESS: _192 Hometown Street, Moneytown, OH 99909_
PHONE NUMBER: _(101) 555-9876_
JOB LOCATION: _192 Hometown Street, Moneytown, OH 99909_

DESCRIPTION OF WORK

Presto Paint will supply, and/or coordinate, all labor and material for the above referenced job as follows:

(1) Supply and install off-white latex paint in the living room, dining room, and family room.
(2) Paint all walls & ceilings and window, door, and base trim.
(3) Paint will be sprayed onto wall and ceiling surfaces, in a manner to properly cover these areas.
(4) Owner may select the off-white color of their choice from and of contractor's suppliers.
(5) Contractor will supply plastic to cover the floor in work areas.
(6) Contractor will prepare all surfaces for paint and scrape all areas, as needed, before painting.
(7) Contractor will remove excess paint from window glass.
(8) All work shall be completed in a timely and workmanlike manner.

No other agreements, whether implied or made verbally, shall be binding.

PAYMENT SCHEDULE

PRICE: _One thousand, eight hundred dollars, ($1,850.00)_ , payable one third _$ 600.00_ due at the signing of the contract, one third _$ 625.00_ due when materials are delivered, one third _$ 625.00_ due when work is completed.

All payments shall be made, in full, upon presentation of each completed invoice.

(continues)

SAMPLE PROPOSAL (continued)

If payment is not made according to the terms above, Presto Paint will have the following rights and remedies. Presto Paint may charge a monthly service charge of one percent (1%), twelve percent (12%) per year, from the first day default is made. Presto Paint may lien the property where the work has been done. Presto Paint may use all legal methods in the collection of monies owed to Presto Paint. Presto Paint may seek compensation, at the rate of $30.00 per hour, for attempts made to collect unpaid monies. Presto Paint may seek payment for legal fees and other costs of collection, to the full extent the law allows.

If the job is not ready for the service or material requested, as scheduled, and the delay is not due to Presto Paint's actions, Presto Paint may charge the customer for lost time. This charge will be at a rate of $30.00 per hour, per man, including travel time.

If you have any questions or don't understand this proposal, seek professional advice. Upon acceptance, this becomes a binding contract between both parties.

Respectfully submitted,

B. D. Contractor
Owner

ACCEPTANCE

We the undersigned do hereby agree to, and accept, all the terms and conditions of this proposal. We fully understand the terms and conditions, and hereby consent to enter into this contract.

Presto Paint _____   Customer _____

By _____

Title _____   Date _____

*PROPOSAL EXPIRES IN 30 DAYS IF NOT ACCEPTED BY ALL PARTIES

have a solid contract. If you agree to have the work done in a time-and-material (T&M) manner, you are responsible for paying whatever the final bill may be. Labor rates can be very deceiving, even among honest contractors. Contractors work at different speeds and skill levels. This distorts the view hourly rates.

The total charge for time and material billing will be relevant to the speed of the contractor. If Mr. Carpenter only charges $25 per hour but does all the work alone, he can cost you more than Zippy Carpenters, who charge $65 per hour for a crew of men. Material prices in this type of billing can also have wide variances from contractor to contractor. One contractor may only charge 15 percent above his cost, while another could charge 35 percent above cost. When you are not protected by a preestablished, firm quote, these costs are uncontrollable and add up quickly.

Crooked contractors love T&M jobs; they can drag the job out and bleed the consumer. They are masters in the art of working without getting anything done. To the untrained eye they appear to be working hard every hour of the day. In truth, they are going through the motions, putting on their best performance, to impress the consumer and collect as much money as possible.

Some Behavior to Watch Out for on T&M Jobs

- Contractors who meticulously unpack and clean up their tools and materials each day.

- Numerous daily trips: first to purchase extra nails, then to get one more stud, then to the hardware store, you pay for all of this extra time needlessly.

- Inexperienced people pretending to be skilled labor.

- Constant trips back and forth from the work truck to the work area.

- Frequent phone calls while on the clock.

QUOTED PRICES

Without a quoted price and a contract, a contractor can set you up before you know what happened. The job may start smoothly but won't stay that way for long. At first extra charges will be minor; this is the feeling-out stage for unscrupulous remodelers. They bill you for the first phase of completed work according to your understanding and include only a few small extra charges. Then the job suddenly develops unforeseen problems, like my truck did, and the next bill is laden with extra costs. When the final stage arrives, the contractor refuses to patch cracks he created in the living room ceiling from excessive hammering until you pay his outrageous bill in full.

Many contractors will try to convince you that a time-and-material job will save you money. After all, you pay only for what you get. They can't hide exorbitant profits the way a contract price can. Just remember, no one does remodeling work without financial reimbursement. You have to decide whether to gamble on a T&M basis or a solid contract. I recommend the firm contract.

There are very few jobs competent contractors cannot give you a firm price on. Once work is started, a contractor has potential lien rights against your property. You cannot compare time-and-material estimates, and they do not give you any information to finalize your budget. Avoid potential problems by keeping a tight leash on the contractor with a firm contract and quoted price.

Avoid dilemmas. Remodeling comes with enough challenges; you don't need to add to them. Stop the problems before they start. Subcontractors aren't the only people who use low bids as a ploy. Material suppliers can be guilty of similar tactics. Envision going to a building supplier to order your kitchen cabinets. After looking at the displays and catalogs, you make your choice, and the company gives you a written estimate. The price looks good, and you order the cabinets. The salesperson tells you the cabinets should be available for delivery in four to six weeks. You rush home to get the remodelers going. In just a few weeks your dream kitchen will be a reality. Or will it?

SAMPLE REMODELING CONTRACT

RICHARD & RHONDA SMART
180 HOMEOWNER LANE
WIZETOWN, OH 99897
(102) 555-6789

REMODELING CONTRACT

This agreement, made this 12th day of May, 2004, shall set forth the whole agreement, in its entirety, between Contractor and Homeowner Contractor: Generic General Contractors, referred to herein as Contractor. Owner: Richard and Rhonda Smart, referred to herein as Homeowner.

Job name: Smart Kitchen Remodel

Job location: 180 Homeowner Lane, Wizetown, OH

The Homeowner and Contractor agree to the following:

SCOPE OF WORK

Contractor shall perform all work as described below and provide all material to complete the work described below:

All work is to be completed by Contractor in accordance with the attached plans and specifications. All material is to be supplied by Contractor in accordance with attached plans and specifications. Said attached plans and specifications have been acknowledged and signed by Homeowner and Contractor.

A brief outline of the work is as follows, this work is only part of the work, and all work referenced in the attached plans and specifications will be completed to the Homeowner's satisfaction. The following is only a basic outline of the overall work to be performed:

REMOVE EXISTING KITCHEN CABINETS
REMOVE EXISTING KITCHEN FLOOR COVERING AND UNDERLAYMENT
REMOVE EXISTING KITCHEN SINK AND FAUCET
REMOVE EXISTING COUNTERTOP
REMOVE EXISTING ELECTRICAL FIXTURES, SWITCHES, AND OUTLETS
REMOVE EXISTING KITCHEN WINDOW
SUPPLY AND INSTALL NEW KITCHEN CABINETS
SUPPLY AND INSTALL NEW KITCHEN SINK AND FAUCET
SUPPLY AND INSTALL NEW KITCHEN UNDERLAYMENT AND FLOOR COVERING
SUPPLY AND INSTALL NEW KITCHEN COUNTERTOP

(page 1 of 4 initials _____)

SAMPLE REMODELING CONTRACT (continued)

SUPPLY AND INSTALL NEW ELECTRICAL FIXTURES, SWITCHES, AND OUTLETS
SUPPLY AND INSTALL NEW KITCHEN GREENHOUSE WINDOW
PATCH, SAND, PRIME AND PAINT WALLS, CEILING, AND TRIM
COMPLETE ALL WORK IN STRICT COMPLIANCE WITH ATTACHED PLANS AND
SPECIFICATIONS, ACKNOWLEDGED BY ALL PARTIES.

COMMENCEMENT AND COMPLETION SCHEDULE

The work described above shall be started within three days of verbal notice from Homeowner, the projected start date is 6/20/04. The Contractor shall complete the above work, in a professional and expedient manner, by no later than twenty days from the start date. Time is of the essence regarding this contract. No extension of time will be valid without the Homeowner's written consent. If Contractor does not complete the work in the time allowed, and if the lack of completion is not caused by the Homeowner, the Contractor will be charged One Hundred Dollars, ($100.00), per day, for every day work is not finished, beyond the completion date. This charge will be deducted from any payments due to the Contractor for work performed.

CONTRACT SUM

The Homeowner shall pay the Contractor for the performance of completed work, subject to additions and deductions, as authorized by this agreement or attached addendum. The Contract Sum is Ten Thousand Three Hundred Dollars, ($10,300.00).

PROGRESS PAYMENTS

The Homeowner shall pay the Contractor installments as detailed below, once an acceptable insurance certificate has been filled by the Contractor, with the Homeowner:

Homeowner will pay Contractor a deposit of One Thousand Five Hundred Dollars ($1,500.00), when demolition work is started.

Homeowner will then pay Two Thousand Dollars, ($2,000.00), when all demolition and rough-in work is complete.

Homeowner will pay Three Thousand Dollars, ($3,000.00), when walls have been painted, and cabinets, countertops, and flooring have been installed.

(page 2 of 4 initials _____)

SAMPLE REMODELING CONTRACT (continued)

Homeowner will pay Three Thousand, Two Hundred Dollars (3,200.00) when all work is complete. Homeowner will pay the final Five Hundred Fifty Dollars ($550.00) within thirty days of completion, if no problems occur and are left uncorrected.

All payments are subject to a site inspection and approval of work by the Homeowner. Before final payment, the Contractor, if required, shall submit satisfactory evidence to the Homeowner, that all expenses, related to this work have been paid and no lien risk exists on the subject property.

WORKING CONDITIONS

Working hours will be 8:00 a.m. through 4:30 a.m., Monday through Friday. Contractor is required to clean their work debris from the job site on a daily basis, and leave the site in a clean and neat condition. Contractor shall be responsible for removal and disposal of all debris related to their job description.

CONTRACT ASSIGNMENT

Contractor shall not assign this contract or further subcontract the whole of this subcontract without the written consent of the Homeowner.

LAWS, PERMITS, FEES, AND NOTICES

Contractor is responsible for all required laws, permits, fees, or notices, required to perform the work stated herein.

WORK OF OTHERS

Contractor shall be responsible for any damage caused to existing conditions. This shall include work performed on the project by other contractors. If the Contractor damages existing conditions or work performed by other contractors, said Contractor shall be responsible for the repair of said damages. These repairs may be made by the Contractor responsible for the damages or another contractor, at the sole discretion of Homeowner.

The damaging Contractor shall have the opportunity to quote a price for the repairs. The Homeowner is under no obligation to engage the damaging Contractor to make the repairs.

(page 3 of 4 initials _____)

SAMPLE REMODELING CONTRACT (continued)

If a different contractor repairs the damage, the Contractor causing the damage may be back charged for the cost of the repairs. These charges may be deducted from any monies owed to the damaging Contractor by the Homeowner.

If no money is owed to the damaging Contractor, said Contractor shall pay the invoiced amount, from the Homeowner, within seven business days. If prompt payment is not made, the Homeowner may exercise all legal means to collect the requested monies.

The damaging Contractor shall have no rights to lien the Homeowner's property for money retained to cover the repair of damages caused by the Contractor. The Homeowner may have the repairs made to their satisfaction.

WARRANTY

Contractor warrants to the Homeowner all work and materials for one year from the final day of work performed.

INDEMNIFICATION

To the fullest extent allowed by law, the Contractor shall indemnify and hold harmless the Homeowner and all of their agents and employees from and against all claims, damages, losses and expenses.

This Agreement entered into on May 12, 2004 shall constitute the whole agreement between Homeowner and Contractor.

_____   _____
Homeowner   Contractor

(page 4 of 4 initials _____)

There are already many potential problems in this example. You ordered your cabinets, and the remodelers are working. A few weeks later, the old cabinets, countertop, and kitchen sink are ripped out. This doesn't bother you, because the new cabinetry will be installed next week. A couple of days without kitchen facilities are tolerable; you have a good excuse to enjoy dining in restaurants. Acting as the general contractor, you've successfully coordinated the remodeling effort flawlessly to this point. You feel great, and the money you've saved by being the general contractor allows some extra features in the new kitchen. You can envision that beautiful, decorative sink and faucet you craved gracing your kitchen ensemble.

The big day arrives. Your new cabinets will come today and by tonight you can do dishes again. By late morning you are getting concerned. By midafternoon you're getting angry. Where are those cabinets? The carpenter and the plumber are waiting for the delivery, and paying them to stand around is eating up your profits. You call the supplier, and a counterperson gets on the phone. When you ask about the status of your cabinet delivery, you are put on hold; the counterperson has to check with the shipping department. The longer you are on hold, the higher your blood pressures gets. This is ridiculous; how hard could it be to give you a delivery time? When the counterperson finally comes back to the phone, you wish she hadn't.

Your cabinets had to be back-ordered and won't be in for a few more weeks. That's the breaking point; now you lose your temper! You demand to speak to the manager, but she is on a break and not available. You hang up, and rush out of the house, leaving the plumber and carpenter waiting for your return. You race to the supplier with your estimate in hand and go straight to the administrative offices. The manager is on the phone. You wait. Anger is now building to a dangerous level. Finally she invites you into the office. You're so upset that when you show her the estimate sheet, it is shaking in your hand. Trying to maintain composure, you explain what is happening to you.

The manager reviews the estimate. You notice a strange expression on her face. When you ask what she intends to do about this, you are astounded. She explains that this estimate is all she has to work with. The details in the estimate are not very good, and tracking the order could be a problem. She goes on to apologize for the present problem and offers to do whatever she can to find your cabinets. In the meantime you have a carpenter and a plumber waiting at your house. The clock is running, and they are expensive. When you ask what can be done about the cabinets, the answer is not what you want to hear. You are given numerous reasons for your problem:

- The estimate is ambiguous.

- Your paperwork doesn't state a delivery date.

- The design of the cabinets isn't detailed in the paperwork.

- Was a countertop ordered?

- The hardware for the doors and drawers is not included with this brand of cabinets. The hardware is a separate order and will take another week or so to get.

- Were you going to pick the cabinets up? There is no reference to delivery in the estimate. Delivery is available, but there is an additional charge for the service.

- Freight charges are not included in the estimate and they are extensive; the cabinets are coming from 1,800 miles away.

This is where the supplier turns your adversity into her advantage. The manager reviews the situation and offers you a deal on cabinets she has in stock. She wants to make amends for your inconvenience. The cabinets in stock retail for 45 percent more than the units you ordered. As compensation for your trouble, she offers you the more expensive cabinets at a discount and will give you free delivery today. The total cost will only be 30 percent more than the original estimate. Since you must incur additional expenses and time delays for the original cabinets, you will save money and time with this deal.

In the example of missing cabinets, if you order cabinets from another supplier, you may have to wait for another month or more. If you wait for your original order, the additional costs will push your losses over the price of the special of the day. What are you going to do? Don't forget about the carpenter and plumber waiting for you and the cabinets at home.

Believe it or not, some companies make their profits from scenarios such as this. Normally, if the building-supply manger is a good salesperson, you will take delivery of the higher-priced cabinets. This is a prime example of the pain that can result from working with loose estimates. Don't do it; get firm quotes.

Now you know the problems with estimates and can recognize the need for written quotes. Even with a general contractor you will need a written quote. If your agreement is in writing, you know what you are paying for and how much it will cost. This is a crucial aspect of any remodeling project. If you allotted $8,300 for cabinets and they wind up costing over $10,000, your out-of-pocket expense has increased considerably. Where will the additional

Use detailed contracts with enforceable clauses, and leave nothing to speculation. As a friend once told me, "There is never a problem until there is a problem."

money come from? You will be forced to take shortcuts and reduce the quality or quantity of the work. Getting into this difficult situation can be avoided with detailed quotes.

The document that will save you time, money, and frustration goes by many names: quote, bid, proposal, or contract; regardless of the term, this is the written instrument you're looking for.

Your Company Name
Your Company Address
Your Company Phone and Fax Numbers

LETTER SOLICITING MATERIAL QUOTES

Date:

Dear:

I am soliciting bids for the work listed below, and I would like to offer you the opportunity to participate in the bidding. If you are interested in giving quoted prices on material(s) for this job, please let me hear from you at the above address.

The job will be started in _____ days/weeks. Financing has been arranged and the job will be starting on schedule. Your quote, if you choose to enter one, must be received no later than

_____.
The proposed work is as follows:

_____

_____

_____

Plans and specifications for the work are available upon request. Thank you for your time and consideration in this request.

Sincerely,

Your Name
Title

Benefits of Quotes

- Quotes contain much more information than estimates.

- Contractors know a quote is a firm price, so they will be much more specific in their description of labor and materials.

- The intent of a quote is to guarantee a fixed price.

- The cost of the service or material cannot exceed the amount specified in the quote.

- Quotes make it easier to maintain your budget.

- When you are dealing with quotes, you can be sure of your costs.

Establish your budget based on the average bid price from several bidders. This will protect you from a low quote that can't be performed. To establish the average price of five different bids, add the total of each proposal together and divide the grand total by the number of bids (in this case five).

> Quotes that are way below average should arouse suspicion. There has to a reason why one price is so much lower than the others. Perhaps you will be unable to get the contractor to do the work when you need it, or the material may not be available during your timetable. These complications force you to consider the next lowest bidder. By using the average quoted price, you won't be placed in a financial bind.

BID REQUESTS

When requesting bids, give all bidders the same information. You cannot expect competitive proposals, if the bidders are working with different information.

Making Bid Requests

- Your bid requests needs to include specific details.

- Complete plans and specifications should accompany the bid requests.

> When requesting bids, give all bidders the same information. You cannot expect competitive proposals, if the bidders are working with different information.

Your Company Name
Your Company Address
Your Company Phone and Fax Numbers

BID REQUEST

Contractor's name: _____

Contractor's address: _____

Contractor's city/state/zip: _____

Contractor's phone number: _____

Job location: _____

Plans and specifications dated: _____

Bid requested from: _____

Type of work: _____

Description of material to be quoted: _____

_____

_____

_____

All quotes to be based on attached plans and specifications. No substitutions allowed without written consent of customer.

Please provide quoted prices for the following: _____

_____

_____

_____

_____

_____

All bids must be submitted by: _____

- You want to establish consistency.

- The prices you get from five contractors should be for exactly the same work.

- Bidders may notice something you left off your plans or specifications. If so, ask them to note any items you omitted as an addendum to the bid.

- If you don't use the procedure outlined here, your bids will not be equal or fair to compare.

A contractor who includes code requirements that you over-looked will be more expensive than a contractor bidding strictly by your plans and specs. In the end, you have to pay for the code requirements; the difference is in knowing the cost before the job is started. You can use the bid process to locate supe-rior contractors. Make note of those who mentioned your omis-sion and those who did not. The contractor who considers aspects and requirements that you did not specify exhibits the extra effort and knowledge to give you a thorough job.

Preparing your bid requests deserves a lot of attention. The bidders will only be obligated to provide costs for the work you specify. This is where all the time and effort you put into your plans and specifications will pay off. Following a few rules in the bidding process will increase your savings.

Don't allow suppliers to substi-tute materials in their bid. Specifi-cations lose their purpose when sub-stitutions are made. If substitutions are mandatory, have them placed on a separate bid addendum. Uniformity in the bids is essential to compare competitive bids.

Specify the grade of lumber to be used. Studs come in several grades. You don't have to require the best, but specify the grade. There is a great deal of difference in the cost between lumber grades. The same is true for other items. If your specifications simply call for sheathing behind your siding, what will your bids be based on? One con-tractor will bid plywood for sheathing. Another may plan to use wafer board. The third contractor might base his quote on

BID ADDENDUM
REQUEST FOR SUBSTITUTIONS

CUSTOMER NAME: Mr. & Mrs. J. P. Homeowner

CUSTOMER ADDRESS: 192 Hometown Street

CUSTOMER CITY/STATE/ZIP: Yooho City, NA 93001

CUSTOMER PHONE NUMBER: (000) 756-3333

JOB LOCATION: Same

PLANS & SPECIFICATIONS DATED: June 10, 2004

BID REQUESTED FROM: Mid Range Suppliers

SUPPLIER ADDRESS: 42 Supplier Street

CONTACT PERSON: Liz Materialwoman, Manager

DATE: July 25, 2004

TYPE OF WORK: Remodeling

THE FOLLOWING ITEMS ARE BEING SUBSTITUTED FOR THE ITEMS SPECIFIED IN THE ATTACHED PLANS AND SPECIFICATIONS:

Roof shingles-The brand specified is not readily available. Our proposed substitute is product number 2246 form WXYZ company. The type, color, and general characteristics are very similar.

Siding-The brand requested is not available through our distribution network. It can be special ordered, but this requires payment prior to order placement. A proposed substitute is product number 4456 from ABEC company. The color and general features are essentially the same as the requested siding.

| Contractor | Date | Customer | Date |

using fiberboard, and a fourth contractor may quote insulated foam sheathing. All the contractors included a price for sheathing, but the prices are all different. It will be easy to tell which bid is lower, but which one is the better value? You have to specify everything to get truly competitive bids.

How To Build Comprehensive Specifications

- Read one of the many books available on the subject.
- Ask professionals for suggestions.
- Call various suppliers and ask them for recommendations on the materials you should use.
- Ask contractors what they normally use in projects similar to your job.
- Surf the Internet for ideas and specifications.
- Read magazines that are aimed at your type of home improvement.

The specifications will take a long time to complete and may feel like a waste of time. You will get bored and confused. After hours of writing specifications, you'll know why architects charge so much. This part will not be as much fun as designing the job. The specifications are as important as or even more important than the design. Spend time at your desk solving problems before they happen. As unpleasant as this job is, it's better than the potential problems you will encounter without dependable specifications.

The result of detailed plans and specifications is a quality quote. You can easily compare all the prices equally and know, without a doubt, what is included in each bid. Compare all bids on a step-by-step basis. If you use a form, such as a bid request form, this is an easy task. All the elements of the quotes are broken down on a bid request sheet. You can scan the page and see every expense to determine who has the best prices on which items. This is another area with the strong potential for saving money.

Putting your job out to bid can be done in several ways. The most common is to request a lump sum price. This method indicates who has the lowest overall price, but it doesn't show you the items that could be bought cheaper elsewhere. Using a detailed bid sheet will expose these savings. Some suppliers will resist detailed bids. They may want to mask their prices in a bulk figure. If they want the sale badly enough, they will comply with your request. If they are unwilling to show you all their prices, you should not deal with them anyway. They are all but telling you that they are hiding something.

Many contractors and homeowners prefer to deal with one supplier. This is definitely the easiest way to buy but not always the best. You might do better by shopping with multiple suppliers.

Contractor's quotes can be challenged in much the same way as those of a supplier can. Request a breakdown of labor and material. Some contractors will not give this information, knowing it could expose excessive hidden profits. If you are suspicious, demand a breakdown. This is the only way to verify quotes and control your costs.

When you go to a grocery store, everything is priced individually. Hardware stores price their items; why should a building supplier be any different? Just because they deal in larger items and higher volume doesn't give them the right to hide their prices. Be firm on this point. Insist on knowing what all the components of your job will cost. It's very easy to hide excessive profits on volume sales. It is not feasible to price every screw, hinge, and nail, but you can price all the major items. Break the items down into bid phases. Phase breakdowns are bargaining chips and can hold hidden treasure for you.

A common trick of the trade is to camouflage material substitutions. This is done by including vague language in a quote, which specifies that your product or "an equal" will be used. Who is to determine what is equivalent to your product? Your satisfaction may not be met with these so-called equal products. Require the bids to be based on specific names, model numbers, colors, and other pertinent information, and you will eliminate these sneaky substitutions.

Reviewing a Bid Sheet

- When you get your prices back, lay the bid sheets beside each other and scan the categories.

- You are sure to find some interesting differences.

- The bottom line will show the overall low bidder.

- The phase prices will expose ways to increase your savings.

- Look at the framing lumber section; who is the overall low bidder on the framing prices?

- How do the window and door prices compare with other suppliers?

- Does their insulation price beat the other bidders?

- What do their numbers look like for the roofing phase?

Use your bid sheets as a negotiating tool.

By now you will have found areas to investigate. The overall low bidder won't be the lowest in all phases. It would be very unusual if one supplier had the lowest prices for every aspect of the job.

SELECTIVE SHOPPING

Selective shopping saves money. You don't have to buy everything from one supplier, but it is best to buy each complete phase from the same company. Don't spend a lot of time buying a little here and little there. Concentrate on the phases and buy from the lowest bidder in each category. Show the other bids to the supplier you prefer. When you put their competitors' prices in front of them, they may offer you a better price. Suppliers price their material in different levels and have room to offer additional discounts.

You won't get a better price if you don't ask for it. Laying your bid sheets on a supplier's counter proves that you are serious. The supplier knows you can and might buy from a competitor. When you get to this stage, you will have their attention. Don't deal with a sales associate; ask to talk with the manager. Only the manger has the ability to give you the lowest price. When the prices are close, you will almost always win. The supplier has invested time and money in preparing your bid and knows the only way to recover the money is by making a sale. You are the buyer and you have power in this negotiation.

> Use your power to save on your material costs. The slower the economy, the better your chances are of winning. Don't be intimidated; it's your money and your decision where to spend it.

Similar tactics work with contractors, especially general contractors. Ask them to segregate their bids into phases and compare the different areas. When you find specific areas with inflated prices, start your negotiations. If a general contractor believes he will lose the entire job because his flooring price is high, he will lower the price to secure the work. The general contractor may ask his subcontractor to lower the price of the work, or he may absorb the loss to be awarded the job. In either event, you benefit from additional savings.

> You need to formulate a plan to have as many bidders compete on the job as possible. The more quotes you get, the better your chances are of saving money. Seek prices from every available source.

Putting your work out to bids will require time; allow several weeks for the process. Many contractors and suppliers will be slow in responding to your request for quotes. Some will refuse to bid the job under your terms and conditions. To get the most for your money, you may have to shop in other areas.

Your Company Name
Your Company Address
Your Company Phone and Fax Numbers

LETTER SOLICITING BIDS FROM SUBCONTRACTORS

Date: _____
Subcontractor address: _____

_____

_____

Dear: _____

I am soliciting bids for the work listed below, and I would like to offer you the opportunity to participate in the bidding. If you are interested in giving quoted prices for the <u>LABOR / MATERIAL</u> for this job, please let me hear from you. The job will start _____. Financing has been arranged and the job will be started on schedule. Your quote, if you choose to enter one, must be received no later than _____.

The proposed work is as follows:

_____

_____

_____

_____

Thank you for your time and consideration in this request.

Sincerely,

Your Name
Title

QUERY FORM LETTER

Dear Sir:

I am soliciting bids for the work listed below, and would like to offer you the opportunity to participate in the bidding. If you are interested in giving quoted prices for the _LABOR/MATERIAL_ for this job, please let me hear from you at the above address. The job will be started _____. Financing has been arranged and the job will be started on schedule. Your quote, if you choose to enter one, must be received no later than _____.

The proposed work is as follows:

_____

_____

_____

_____

Thank you for your time and consideration in this request.

Sincerely,

Large cities can afford you lower prices. In some cases you may find out-of-state prices are lower. Maine's material prices are high; I can buy the exact same products in Massachusetts for up to 35 percent less. You may find similar savings with your exploratory bid requests. Take the time to conduct the bid process properly. It is your best shot at saving money.

To save time, solicit bids by mail and include a complete bid package with each request. To save on copying and postage costs, start with a letter. Send a letter to each prospective bidder to see if they are interested in bidding your work. When you get favorable replies, mail the complete package. You will be surprised by how much you can save with aggressive shopping.

Tips for Serious Negotiations

- When you get into serious negotiations, watch your step.
- Don't be fooled by low prices based on substituted materials.
- Confirm, in writing, the delivery and completion dates.
- Beware of any bidder beating all the others by a large margin. All the bids should be within the same range; if one is substantially lower, something is wrong.
- Double-check your plans and specifications before requesting quotes.
- Once you receive the quotes, you can begin to eliminate contractors and suppliers; then you will be ready to negotiate for the best possible deal.

Obtaining solid bid prices is crucial to your job, so invest the time required to do it right. Once you have your bids, you are ready to move to the next phase. Every step along the remodeling and improvement road can be a key move.

5

Negotiating Your Best Deal

You can save big money with the right techniques. These savings are especially evident on larger jobs. The more you are buying or contracting for, the more you can save. Contractors and suppliers rarely give you their lowest price. They are in business to make money and will not voluntarily discount any more than necessary to win the job. Getting to the bottom line will take time and planning on your part. Your efforts will be compensated with meaningful savings.

As a consumer, it can be difficult to recognize inflated prices. You have very little to compare prices with, and most comparisons come from the same type of sources. All of these sources are looking to make money and increase the list price of their materials accordingly. How will you know when you have reached your best deal? Getting to the lowest price is a matter of trial and error. You have to keep negotiating until you are at a standstill. By using special tactics, you can be more successful than most consumers. These strategies will be explained in detail throughout this chapter.

SAVINGS

Suppliers offer you the most opportunity for savings. They price materials in different levels, and as a homeowner you will be given the highest prices of all. The average homeowner accepts this and pays the premium price. If you negotiate, you can save a minimum of 10 percent. The savings can be much larger, because various items carry different percentages of mark-up.

Some of the items with the highest mark-ups are the ones you are most likely to use. These products include kitchen cabinets, plumbing fixtures, light fixtures, and other finish items. Lumber and basic construction materials fluctuate in the percentage of mark-up, as do windows and doors. Almost any expensive item will have a large profit built into the price. Wholesale prices vary as much as 30 percent, and average consumer mark-ups run from 10 percent to 50 percent. This means that there is a big spread in the prices you might pay for identical materials. Buying from the right place can reduce your costs by an average of 15 percent.

The products with the highest mark-ups are frequently light fixtures. Lights carry price increases of up to 100 percent above what an electrical contractor pays. Why do light fixtures support such a large mark-up compared to plumbing fixtures, which have a 25 percent mark-up? Most light fixtures are low dollar items, allowing for a larger retail mark-up. Excessive mark-up on an already costly whirlpool, for example, would reduce its market appeal. No one questions the $50 price of a light fixture that wholesales for $25. This seems a small expense when compared to the $8,500 it will cost to remodel your bathroom.

As a contractor I have seen the contractor's prices and compared them to retail price tags on light fixtures. They frequently carry a 75 percent or higher mark-up. Obviously, if an electrical supplier wants to make a sale, there is room to negotiate a lower price. Sometimes all you have to do is ask for a lower price, but there are occasions when you must be a tough negotiator.

The next phase to look at is plumbing. Plumbing fixtures are a good category to scrutinize. In some areas only licensed plumbers can buy direct from wholesale dealers. In other locations you can buy from wholesale dealers but only at retail prices. Try to get prices for the same products from both your plumber and a supplier. There is no way of knowing who will give you a better price until you compare them side-by-side.

Some plumbing contractors sell their fixtures considerably above the suggested list price. Others let you have the material at 10 percent above their cost. They do this to win the overall bid and make a profit from their standard hourly labor rate. On items over $200, the average mark-up to you from a plumber will be between 10 percent and 35 percent. On less expensive items the percentage may be as high as 100 percent.

Plumbing fixtures purchased directly from a supplier will carry average mark-ups from 20 percent to 50 percent above wholesale. The brand and price range of the item are the determining factors in the mark-up. A toilet could have a mark-up of about 75 percent, and a standard bathtub will carry a profit percentage of about 45 percent. Inexpensive wall-hung lavatories can be marked up 65 percent, and well pumps can have profit margins of 100 percent. The kitchen faucet you pay $95 for will cost the plumber around $58. More expensive items, such as whirlpools, carry mark-ups in the 25 percent range. Armed with this knowledge, you can whittle away at plumbing profit margins during the negotiation process.

> Don't hesitate to ask contractors and suppliers for lower prices. At worst, the price will not be lowered. What do you have to lose? Try to get the best deal possible.

Heating systems carry mark-ups in the 40-percent level. Don't overlook heating accessories while campaigning for a lower price on the main heating unit. HVAC accessories can be sold at profits as high as 100 percent. As a savvy consumer work all the angles in achieving the lowest prices possible. Furnace and boiler prices are worth negotiating, but the big savings are in the accessories. The contractor may sell the main heating system at only 20 percent above his cost but will undermine your budget with the parts that go with it. Thermostats, valves, and similar items may be marked up by 75 percent or more. Ask for a detailed break-down of all labor and materials.

Most contractors will try to avoid giving itemized break-downs of their prices. The first strategy might be to show you the actual invoice on the biggest product. They will explain that they are only marking the unit up by 20 percent. The con-tractor will try to justify the need for this with overhead expenses. These expenses include delivery, paperwork, and insurance. All of this will make sense and sound reasonable, which is the purpose of showing you the figures. The con-tractor's attempt to justify the profit margin is to get you to agree that the mark-ups are fair.

Most strict investigation from consumers ends here. The ploy is to convince you that the prices are fair. Once you see the actual invoice on a product, you are expected to admit the price is rational. While the mark-up on the main unit is fair, contractors can fleece you with little items. The majority of contractors will not be trying to take advantage of you. Only a few will resort to these unsavory sales tactics. They put your suspicions to rest with the big-ticket item and empty your wallet with the accessories. Most homeowners stop asking ques-tions after seeing the actual invoice on the most expensive item. This is where they make their big mistake.

> Don't accept evidence of prices for one or two items; require a detailed breakdown on all labor and materials.

Basic construction products are the hardest to save on. Dry-wall, paint, lumber, and related items offer mark-ups in the 10 percent to 20 percent range. These percentages are lower, but the volume of materials used will justify negotiating. You will use more of these items than anything else. Do not be blinded by the relatively small percentages of profit. Spend enough time shopping to be sure you are getting the best deals available. Saving 5 percent on all the lumber and drywall used to build your addition will make a huge difference in the price.

Carpet and vinyl are marked up by as much as 75 percent. All the subtle little extras such as stain resistance, no wax, and associated terms add to the price. There are several grades and types of flooring to choose from.

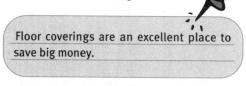

Floor coverings are an excellent place to save big money.

Ceramic tile floors give contractors a hefty mark-up on materials. You can beat these prices at tile outlet centers and through negotiation.

Kitchen cabinets and countertops are another area to attack. The profit percentage here can easily exceed 60 percent, with mark-ups on custom cabinets being even higher. Kitchen appliances cost the contractor 10 percent to 15 percent less than the typical consumer. These items may not be worth your time and trouble, depending on what your time is worth. Special

> Research your costs and compare them to the contractor's material quote. Remember to allow for delivery charges if you supply the materials yourself. By investing your time, the savings can mount up.

kitchen items carry the largest mark-ups. Objects such as garden- style windows have absurd profits built into the sale price. The same is true of unique sinks and faucets. With any of these items save money with thrifty shopping and supply the product yourself.

Insulation isn't worth your time. The mark-ups are low and the savings are minimal. Hire subcontractors to supply and install the insulation. In some cases you cannot buy the material for the price a contractor charges to supply and install it. Many people experience skin irritations from insulation. Unless you enjoy working for minimal savings and getting very itchy, avoid doing your own insulation. It is just not worth the effort.

Windows and doors are a different story. Depending upon the brand, the mark-up can hit 65 percent. This amounts to a lot in an addition full of windows. Make the supplier sharpen her pencil on the window and door prices; there is plenty of room for discounts here. Beat the supplier's lowest price and supply your own windows and doors. You'll be glad you did.

Avoid buying "Special Purchase" windows. These are often seconds that have production flaws in them. The sizes could be off, or the windows may leak air. The money that you save with some special-purchase windows is not worth what you give up.

Standard trim lumber does not offer much room for savings, but custom-milled trim material does. If you are going with standard trim, let the subcontractor supply it. Most of what you lose will be headaches. On the other hand, wallpaper is an excellent source of savings. It carries a profit ranging from 45 percent to 100 percent. By now you're getting the picture. There are certain areas to focus on when seeking lower prices. Now that you know what to save on, you must learn how to achieve those savings.

The first "give-away discount" is from an inflated price; never accept this as the best you can do. Strive for the absolute best savings you can obtain through relentless negotiations.

Is there a golden rule to obtaining maximum savings? Every seller will respond to a different approach. The direct approach works with some vendors; simply asking for a better price can produce good results. Many estimators build a "give away" factor into their quote. For some this will take the form of a cash discount. Others will offer you an upgraded product for the same price as a less expensive item. In either case these aren't real savings. Yes, they are a saving from the original quote, but there is still more to save.

I have found the best approach with material suppliers is to put numbers in front of them. To get the lowest price, you need to have your facts together and be ready to make a commitment. After collecting several bids from suppliers, you're ready to play the game. This is like playing poker, but, because you already hold the winning hand, you show your cards to the other players. Use your bid request sheet, which breaks down the different phases of the job to enter various suppliers' prices. Listing them side-by-side creates a strong graphic. When a supplier sees the competition's prices, it has a hard-hitting effect.

Sit down with the manager of the building-supply store and show her where her prices are too high. Stress your interest in buying all your material from her company. Then ask her to reconsider the store's original quote. The odds are good that you will be offered reduced pricing. If you aren't, pack up your bid request sheet and visit the other suppliers. Don't be haughty or rude to any of the managers; you may have to deal with them later.

I have priced my material 20 percent below my competitors and still made more money than they did. This was possible because of aggressive shopping. A savings of 20 percent on materials amounts to major money, and homeowners have the same option to save money through serious shopping. If you act as your own general contractor and find a discount supplier, you could save 30 percent on the total cost of your job. On a $40,000 job, this is a savings of $12,000.

> If you live in a small town, branch out with your savings effort. Call suppliers in the larger cities. Pricing is often more competitive in a larger area with more choices. Cities provide higher populations and higher demand. They also support more building- supply outlets. These factors contribute to lower prices. Many out-of-town suppliers will deliver to your job at no additional cost. It requires extra time to investigate the options, but the savings can be outstanding.

INFLATED MATERIAL PRICES

If you find a contractor with inflated material prices, offer to supply the material yourself. Be prepared for a battle; many contractors will tell you that they don't work with owner-supplied material. Some of their reasons have merit. Frequently owners make mistakes ordering materials, costing the contractor time and money. When a contractor sends a full crew to your house, they are expected to work.

If you make a mistake with the material acquisition, the crews may not be able to work. The same is true, if you receive the wrong or damaged material. Either way, the crews cannot work. This is disappointing to you and devastating to the contractor. Your mistake can cost the contractor $1,200 a day or more. These events happen often enough to make experienced contractors apprehensive.

When they hit you with this objection, take it away. Tell the contractor you will pay extra for any lost time due to your failure to have the correct materials on the job. When you make this offer, be prepared to volley back and forth for control. You have just agreed to put a special clause in the contract to protect the contractor; don't make this agreement completely one-sided in favor of the contractor. The remodeler may request to be compensated an hourly rate for all lost time. If so, this rate should be reasonable and should have an established maximum daily limit.

The contractor might try to require a daily penalty for every mishap you make. While you can understand why contractors need to protect their income from your inexperience, you must remain in control at all times. The contract provisions should not include excessive penalties or compensation. After all, if the shoe was on the other foot, would the contractor agree to pay you $1,000 for every day his material delivery was delayed?

> Do not create a situation where a contractor looks for reasons why his crews cannot work. Keep the contractor motivated to complete the job rather than giving him an opportunity to abuse your bank account.

SCHEDULING

You can protect yourself by scheduling your material deliveries to arrive two days before they will be needed. Agree to pay the contractor a delay fee only if you are unable to give him

---

SAMPLE COMPLETION CLAUSE

COMMENCEMENT AND COMPLETION SCHEDULE

The work described above shall be started within 3 days of verbal notice from the customer, the projected start date is 1/2/04. The Contractor shall complete the above work in a professional and expedient manner by no later than twenty (20) days from the start date. Time is of the essence of this subcontract. No extension of time will be valid without the customer's written consent. If contractor does not complete the work in the time allowed and if the lack of completion is not caused by the customer, the contractor will be charged one hundred dollars ($100.00) for every day after the completion date. This charge will be deducted from any payments due to the contractor for work performed.

---

24 hours' notice of a scheduling change. With this much time, he can change his schedule and not lose money from lack of work the next day. You want to propose a fair agreement to both parties. If the contractor still balks at your offer, you have exposed a greedy contractor. This remodeler is either trying to hide excessive profit in his material prices or wants to milk penalty fees out of you. You may reach a standoff, with no satisfactory solution. If the contractor refuses to price the job based on installing your materials, find another contractor.

> No reputable contractor will refuse to use your materials under the proper conditions. Conversely, be suspicious of a contractor who insists that you supply all the materials. These may be remodeling bandits, setting you up to steal your materials and disappear into another state. Stick to your guns and keep the contractor leveraged into the job. Never pay retail prices for materials and cover all the bases.

When the remodeler is working on a contract price, he or she can't afford lost time. The quicker the job is finished, the more profit is made. If you supply the material, the contractor doesn't have control of the job production time. Your offer to compensate for any lost time removes the contractor's risk of loss. Any continued resistance from the contractor indicates trouble.

Getting contractors to lower their prices is difficult. They can be very independent and stubborn. If you try to supply your own material, some contractors won't do your work because they want the extra profit from material mark-ups. If the contractor you choose is a small operator, he might appreciate owner-supplied material. He will not have to tie up money in materials and won't have to worry about getting paid on time for his materials. Supplying your own material is a great way to cut costs if you can coordinate punctual, accurate deliveries.

LABOR RATES

Negotiating for lower labor rates is the hardest part of the bidding process. Good people won't work cheap. They don't need to. There is a shortage of quality contractors, and superior tradespeople know they are in demand. These contractors know they can maintain their prices and still stay busy. In most cases, it is possible to shave up to 7 percent off the labor quotes without sacrificing the best contractors. Most good remodelers factor in this much to allow for problems.

If this buffer amount is the pivotal point, contractors may forfeit it to secure the job. If they refuse to drop their prices, chances are that you have found a good contractor. These expert tradespeople rarely take a job with the intent of breaking even or losing money. Keep in mind that contractors have overhead expenses and need a fair wage to survive.

Labor is different from material. It doesn't carry the same kind of profit latitude. Material is easy; a supplier buys a sink for a fixed price and sells it for a profit. Labor doesn't work that way. A contractor can never be absolutely sure of the labor cost to do a job. He can't look in a catalog and determine his exact cost. All he can do is draw on his experience to estimate the total labor needed for the project. With remodeling this guesswork is especially difficult. How can you calculate the exact time required to replace kitchen cabinets? Determining the amount of time needed to raise a roof or add a dormer is an exacting process.

When a contractor is dealing with new construction, such as additions, estimates are much easier to make. There are few existing conditions to contend with. The contractor knows what to expect when building a garage and can be comfortable with the hours needed to complete the job. Stripping an existing bathroom to the bare studs and joists is a different story. Estimating the labor in this situation is risky. The best a remodeler can do is to rely on his years of experience and allow for the unexpected by padding the price.

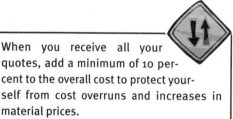

When you receive all your quotes, add a minimum of 10 percent to the overall cost to protect yourself from cost overruns and increases in material prices.

There is no way to know what will be found when the wall coverings are removed. Suppose the floor joists have rotted? Will the existing conditions allow for a satisfactory finish without unplanned additional work? Warped walls or floor joists require additional preparation before the finished products can be applied. On one remodeling job we opened the wall to do a simple sink installation and discovered a swarm of bees. Working in a beekeeper's suit slows your work down quite a bit! A seasoned contractor will have some money loaded into the quote to allow for these unforeseen problems. You can extract this money from the bid and enjoy the savings.

How can you coerce the contractor to eliminate his buffer zone and drop the extra money figured into his price? You can offer guarantees and make your contract contingent on certain circumstances. This technique can save you money and put the contractor at ease. When a reputable remodeler pads a bid, it is to protect against unknown conditions. You can act as an insurance company and play the odds. How often will bathroom floor joists be rotten? Normally there will be evidence to suggest a problem with the floor structure. The floor will slope, the toilet will be unstable, or the baseboard trim will be discolored. Contractors look for these warning signs and you can, too.

In the remodeling game the odds can favor an informed homeowner. This is a strategic mental battle, like chess. When the contractor has given you his best price, make your first move. Ask the contractor what he can do to reduce the price. The contractor will probably claim that he cannot go any lower on the price. Ask if he has included an allowance for unforeseen problems. If the contractor says he doesn't allow extras for problems, find a new contractor. This one is either inexperienced, or he is lying to you. When the contractor admits to an extra cushion in the bid, make your next move. Explain how you understand his need to allow for unexpected problems. Offer to remove this risk from his contract by inserting a clause regarding existing conditions. The clause will protect the contractor from the unexpected.

Removing these risks from the contractor entitles you to a lower price. There is jeopardy involved in an offer of this nature. You are responsible for all costs incurred to correct existing problems. Assess the situation carefully before offering such a proposal. Be aware of the potential costs you may be responsible for. Request a lower price to compensate you for assuming the risks. If the contractor has to be responsible only for known conditions, he can afford to do the job for less. Checkmate, you win. If you are lucky, you will save money, and even if problems occur, you can use your savings to solve them. Weigh your savings against your risks before approaching the contractor with this offer.

You can try to lower a contractor's price by comparing the price to other contractors. In slower economic times this will be an effective tool. If there are more quality contractors than there is work, you are in the power position. In strong economic times you lose this leverage against the remodelers. Even in a poor economy, good remodelers are in demand. Slow economic conditions force people to remodel because they can't afford to buy or sell. These factors make it tough to get a reduced price from remodelers; good remodeler's rates are usually firm. If you can get any discount, you've done a good job.

Every time a contractor bids a job, he is asked the same question, "Is this the best you can do?" Don't begin your negotiations with this obvious lead. Instead, offer to increase the contractor's benefits. Are you dealing with subcontractors in various trades? Here are some tidbits to whet their appetites.

> Making you job attractive to the contractor is the key to bargaining for a lower price.

Tips for Getting Cheaper Rates

- General contractors rarely offer contract deposits to their subs. The accepted business practice is to pay for the job within 30 days of completion. If you are willing to pay promptly, you can demand a lower price.

- Giving a deposit when materials are delivered is another way to make your job appealing.

- Your ability to keep a subcontractor's cash flow at high tide is a powerful motivator.

- Creative scheduling is another trump card you can play. Evaluate your timetable and production needs, then consider allowing the subcontractor to use your job as fill-in work. If your job allows for latitude in completion time, this is a powerful option to exercise.

- Try to get a price break for being conveniently located to an ongoing job that a contractor is working on in your neighborhood.

ASK QUESTIONS

When you start to talk with subcontractors, ask questions about their willingness and availability to do your work. Try to establish their true motivations. If you learn enough about them, you can uncover areas to focus your negotiations. Most general contractors try to beat subcontractors down to their lowest price. Acting as your own general, you can pay the sub more for the job and still make money. You can't compete with the volume offered by established general contractors, but you can successfully win subcontractors away. Your job can offer more money and added benefits. You can negotiate for lower prices without sacrificing quality.

Cutting corners on contractors can become very expensive. Choosing a contractor with the lowest bid could be a major mistake. You have to evaluate the quality of the contractor's work and the caliber of each contractor. When you find the right one, he or she may be expensive. Jockey for the best position possible, but keep in mind that his or her abilities could be well worth the price.

Don't pay a premium price for substandard work and avoid paying full-time rates for part-time production. Beware of part-timers who only do this kind of work for extra money. Moonlighters often work for a fraction of the cost of a full-time contractor. In some rare circumstances this is a good value. More often than not, it is trouble. These occasional contractors seldom have the proper insurance, and many are not licensed. If they were truly good at the trade, they would probably be working for themselves full-time. Part-timers fall into two categories.

The first group is working for extra money, and has no intention of building a business. These contractors are dangerous. You will have no recourse for warranty claims, and they can disappear overnight.

The second group is interested in starting a full-time business. To go into business, you must set aside operating capital. The transition period between full-time employee and full-time business owner is arduous. A delicate balance must be maintained until the change can be made. These would-be contractors can represent your best value. They will give you excellent service because they want to establish references to build their business.

Offer to allow the contractor to use your job as a reference and request a lower price for the privilege. This helps both of you. Your reference provides the contractor with new work, which benefits his business growth. If the contractor is successful in business, he will be there for your future needs. If he is seriously starting a business, the contractor will have licenses and insurance. If he doesn't, don't use him. All the savings in the world are not worth the damages possible with an unlicensed contractor with no insurance.

Concentrate your savings efforts on material. When you are shopping for specific brands and model numbers, it is easy to recognize a good deal. If the two products are identical and delivery is available, the lowest bidder should win. You don't have to use judgement in evaluating the differences in identical materials, since there aren't any. With contractors you cannot be so sure of your decisions. Don't bargain yourself into a bad deal.

> Gambling on evening contractors is playing for high stakes. You can save up to 30 percent with part-time contractors, but you can lose much more. Put the part-timers through the same tests as the full-time contractors. If they pass your tests, protect yourself and proceed with caution. You should save money by using these up-and-coming contractors.

Your goal is to obtain prices that are competitive and realistic. This requires detective work, determination, and the ability to gain the upper hand. Once you sit down at the bargaining table, judge the circumstances and play all of your hole cards. Increased savings are your reward for mastering the challenging game of negotiation.

6

Making Deposit and Installment Payments

Knowing when to advance payments to contractors requires a very delicate balance of authority and acceptance. If you pay too soon, you have no control over the contractor. If you pay too slowly, the contractors will not continue to work for you. Your choice of financing and agreements with contractors and suppliers will govern when payments will be made. The schedule of payments should be described in your contract. Payment terms need to be very specific and should include provisions for your inspection of all material and work before money is advanced.

TERMS

Different contractors will want payment at different times. There are no set rules about when to pay; it is negotiated between you and the contractor. Don't allow a contractor to pressure you into a so-called standard payment plan. There is no such thing. The payment plan you and the contractor agree to will be the acceptable practice. Typical proposals will request a deposit when the contract is signed, which is usually one-third of the total contract price. The next payment is scheduled for the midpoint or rough-in phase of the job. This amount is also one-third of the total contract price. Finally, the last third of the agreed price is due in full upon completion.

Almost any proposal you receive from a contractor will have a payment request similar to this example. For many contractors, this is considered the standard payment schedule. If your job is small, it may be reasonable to break the payments into thirds. A reasonable deposit, with the balance upon completion, would be a better approach for you. Some proposals you receive will request a 50 percent deposit. This is ludicrous even for a small project.

Never consider giving away half the job cost in the form of a deposit. You leave yourself wide open for abuse under these conditions. Try to avoid deposits whenever possible.

If your contractor demands a deposit, keep the deposit at 25 percent of the contract price or less. Some contractors will emphasize the importance of a cash deposit to make the contract binding. Money doesn't have to change hands to make a legal contract. None of the states I have worked in require cash to create a legal agreement.

Most laws only require a promise to establish a binding legal contract. All this means is that the contractor pledges to do the work and you agree to pay for it. Promises of this kind are referred to as valuable consideration. Good and valuable consideration is the standard clause for most legal contracts. Keep as much of your money as possible for as long as possible. Consult your attorney for any legal issues.

Many homeowners are willing to accept a contractor's terms without question. Many people don't realize that they can request a different payment schedule. Since most consumers agree to the routine payment schedule, it can be hard to convince a contractor to consider alternative arrangements. It will be in your best interest to try for different terms. There are several objections to the so-called standard payment

Your Company Name
Your Company Address
Your Company Phone and Fax Numbers

PROPOSAL

Date: _____

Customer name: _____

Address: _____

Phone number: _____

Job location: _____

DESCRIPTION OF WORK

Your Company Name will supply, and/or coordinate, all labor and material for the above referenced job as follows:

_____

_____

_____

_____

PAYMENT SCHEDULE

Price: _____ dollars ($_____)

Payments to be made as follows:

_____

_____

_____

All payments shall be made in full, upon presentation of each completed invoice. If payment is not made according to the terms above, Your Company Name will have the following rights and remedies. Your Company Name may charge a monthly service charge of _____ (_____%) percent, _____ (_____%) percent per year, from the first day default is made. Your Company Name may lien the property where the work has been done. Your Company Name may use all legal methods in the collection of monies owed to it. Your Company Name may seek compensation, at the rate of $_____ per hour, for attempts made to collect unpaid monies.

(Page 1 of 2. Please initial _____.)

PROPOSAL (continued)

Your Company Name may seek payment for legal fees and other costs of collection, to the full extent the law allows.

If the job is not ready for the service or materials requested, as scheduled, and the delay is not due to Your Company Name's actions, Your Company Name may charge the customer for lost time. This charge will be at a rate of $_____ per hour, per man, including travel time.

If you have any questions or don't understand this proposal, seek professional advice. Upon acceptance, this proposal becomes a binding contract between both parties.

Respectfully submitted,

Your Name
Title

ACCEPTANCE

We the undersigned do hereby agree to, and accept, all the terms and conditions of this proposal. We fully understand the terms and conditions, and hereby consent to enter into this contract.

Your Company Name   Customer

By: _____   _____

Title: _____   Date: _____

Date: _____

Proposal expires in 30 days, if not accepted by all parties.

(Page 2 of 2)

schedule. The most important objection is the potential loss of your hard-earned money.

When you hand over your deposit, you may never see it again. The contractor could skip town with your money before you know anything is wrong. This example assumes the worst, but it can and does happen. A less cynical consideration is the risk of the contractor losing his business to pursuing creditors. Relentless collection demands could take your money from the contractor before your job is completed. Now the contractor does not have the money necessary to pay for your job's labor and materials. If the contractor is in trouble, your money is at risk.

What if the business has not paid its taxes? The company will be hit with a tax lien against all its assets, and your deposit money could be considered an asset. This is a serious problem. When a tax lien is applied to the assets of the business, your money is tied up. What assurances do you have of your money being safe? You are vulnerable when giving a deposit.

Another risk is one of misappropriated funds. Remodelers, plagued with debt, often resort to finance juggling. The contractor may take your deposit and use it to pay for another job's material. Even strong companies will limit their operating capital needs by spreading deposit money over several jobs. This is wrong, but it's done all the time. Normally,

> Try to avoid giving contractors money that they have not earned. Don't pay for materials until they are delivered, and never pay for labor before the work is done.

everything works out. It's when plans don't work out that you lose. Of course, you could sue the contractor to recover your deposit, but lawsuits are time-consuming and expensive. If the company is in financial trouble, what will you collect when you finally win the lawsuit? Not much; if a contractor files for bankruptcy, there is almost nothing you can do to recover your money. You will have to take a place in line with all the other homeowners and creditors. Your options are extremely limited by the bankruptcy courts.

Bankruptcy circumstances are the exception rather than the rule. However, there are enough business failures to warrant caution. Keep any deposits given at a minimal amount to reduce your exposure. The deposit should not exceed 25 percent of the contract amount. This is a fair deposit for the contractor, and you have lowered your risk. Do not give a deposit at the time you sign the contract. Authorize the deposit to be paid when materials are delivered and work is started. This approach reduces the amount of time your money is at high risk. If a contractor can't afford to buy materials without your money, he should not be doing your job.

> If something doesn't sound or feel right, pay attention to your instincts. Making a decision about a contractor is a big responsibility. Don't take it lightly. If you suspect that there is a hook in the bait, don't bite it.

Established contractors deal with suppliers on a thirty-day account basis. When they buy materials, they have thirty days to pay for them. Requiring contractors to put materials on the job to initiate the payment schedule is not unreasonable. If they won't comply with this request, look for another contractor.

> I must stress the importance of staying in control of your money and your project. You could easily get hurt financially when doing business with contractors who demand large deposits at the signing of the contract.

LIEN WAIVER

When making any cash advancements, require the recipient to sign a lien waiver. Lien waivers should be required for every service rendered and all materials supplied. There are two types of lien waivers. The first type is called a short-form lien waiver. These are used individually for each cash disbursement to each contractor or supplier. The second style is referred to as a long-form lien waiver. This form combines materials and services and has a place for several signatures. All vendors pro-

Your Company Name
Your Company Address
Your Company Phone and Fax Numbers

SHORT-FORM LIEN WAIVER

Customer name: _____

Customer address: _____

Customer city/state/zip: _____

Customer phone number: _____

Job location: _____

Date: _____

Type of work: _____

Contractor: _____

Contractor address: _____

Subcontractor: _____

Subcontractor address: _____

Description of work completed to date: _____

Payments received to date: _____

Payment received on this date: _____

Total amount paid, including this payment: _____

The contractor/subcontractor signing below acknowledges receipt of all payments stated above. These payments are in compliance with the written contract between the parties above. The contractor/subcontractor signing below hereby states payment for all work done to this date has been paid in full.

The contractor/subcontractor signing below releases and relinquishes any and all rights available to place a mechanic or materialman lien against the subject property for the above described work. All parties agree that all work performed to date has been paid for in full and in compliance with their written contract.

The undersigned contractor/subcontractor releases the general contractor/customer from any liability for nonpayment of material or services extended through this date. The undersigned contractor/subcontractor has read this entire agreement and understands the agreement.

_____   _____
Contractor/Subcontractor   Date

viding labor or materials sign on the same form. The long form is preferred by many attorneys and reduces paperwork. You many find the short form equally if not more effective, especially if your schedule requires payments to different people at different times.

Essentially, these forms state that the vendor receiving your money is releasing your property from the threat of a lien. I cannot stress enough the importance of obtaining these releases. Without lien waivers, you are at the mercy of contractors and suppliers, because any disagreement over payment can result in a lien

Require contractors and suppliers to sign lien waivers when they are paid. This will protect your property from nasty lawsuits.

on your property. There is no minimum requirement for a lien. A company supplying one door for your job has lien rights. Liens are used to secure an unpaid contractor's or supplier's position until the courts render a decision. Liens are costly to remove; they cloud the title to your property; and selling a house with a recorded lien against it is very difficult.

Removing the lien will require payment of the disputed amount or a court decision. The contractor can lien the house for any of the work he has done and not been paid for. To win in court, you will have to prove that you should not have to pay the amount in question. Lien waivers are your best defense. Once the contractor signs the lien waiver, he has no lien rights on the work described in the waiver. Lien waivers become a part of your arsenal of written documentation. If you show evidence of having everything in writing, the contractor's verbal claims will lose credibility. Maintain good records from the start of the job.

Going to court will get expensive fast. Even with a bogus claim, you will have to defend yourself. Your equity and home are at stake; you can't ignore a lien. An aggressive contractor will follow the lien with a lawsuit to perfect the lien. Even if you have paid the contractor, you may have to appear in court to prove it. If you engage attorneys to represent you, they will

Your Company Name
Your Company Address
Your Company Phone and Fax Numbers

LONG-FORM LIEN WAIVER

Customer name: _____

Customer address: _____

Customer city/state/zip: _____

Customer phone number: _____

Job location: _____

Date: _____

Type of work: _____

The vendor acknowledges receipt of all payments stated below. These payments are in compliance with the written contract between the vendor and the customer. The vendor hereby states that payment for all work done to this date has been paid in full.

The vendor releases and relinquishes any and all rights available to said vendor to place a mechanic or materialman lien against the subject property for the described work. Both parties agree that all work performed to date has been paid for, in full and in compliance with their written contract.

The undersigned vendor releases the customer and the customer's property from any liability for nonpayment of material or services extended through this date. The undersigned contractor has read this entire agreement and understands the agreement.

Vendor*	Services	Date Paid	Amount Paid
Plumbing Contractor	Rough-in		
Plumbing Contractor	Final		
Electrician	Rough-in		
Electrician	Final		
Supplier	Framing Lumber		

*This list should include all contractors and suppliers. All vendors are listed on the same lien waiver, and sign above their trade name for each service rendered, at the time of payment.

charge you for all the time they spend on the case. These charges will involve more than actual time in court. The expenses include courtroom preparation and the time spent investigating your claims.

With the proper paperwork, you can avoid courtroom conflicts. Insist on having lien waivers signed by everyone you pay.

Attorney's rates can easily be $150 per hour. Add this to the lost time and money on the job, and any savings you had to this point are rapidly depleted. It doesn't seem fair, but it is a fact.

Often liens are filed as the result of a misunderstanding. The contractor believes he is to be paid a certain amount at a specific time, and the homeowner disagrees. The homeowner may feel it is necessary to withhold payment until problems with the workmanship are corrected. If you do not cover this possibility in your contract and neglect to get lien waivers signed for partial payments, you can lose in court.

You have already put the contractor's profit in his pocket with the first two payments. Any time the contractor has received more money than has been earned, you are asking for trouble. You have relinquished your power position, and the contractor can come to think he is in total control. It is unlikely that you have the remodeling knowledge to anticipate every possible problem or recognize every probable conflict. Everyone gets a fair deal when you establish the rules upfront and in writing.

ADVANCE PAYMENTS

Another problem with the three-part payment schedule is the second advance. When you give the contractor a third for a deposit, he is already working with your money. When you pay the second third of the contract price, the contractor is way ahead financially. Most of the remodeler's profit is gained from the first and second payment. His expenses are covered, and when you make the second payment, he has most of the job's profit in hand. The last payment covers the actual cost of the remaining work but does not include much profit.

Paying in thirds can be a problem with any trade, but mechanical trades are historically the worst offenders. The three-part payment schedule caters to plumbers, electricians, and heating contractors. It is much easier for these mechanical trades to make their profits before completion of a job.

To illustrate this point, let's look at a very realistic scenario. You live in an upper- middle-class community. Your remodeling plans call for adding two new bathrooms and a master bedroom. Since the surrounding homes support large, impressive bathrooms, you want to invest in quality fixtures to get the best return for your dollar. You've also worked hard for this addition and want it to be both enjoyable and profitable. One of the bathrooms will adjoin the new master bedroom, and the other will serve your guests.

When you draw up your plumbing contract, you attach a detailed specification sheet. You do everything by the book. All your bases are covered, and nothing is left to chance. The plumbing contractor looks over your spec sheet and is impressed with your fixture selection. The plumber says he can do the job for $18,000 but will need a deposit when you sign the contract. The deposit request is for $6,000, one-third of the total contract price, which the plumber explains is the standard amount. He insists that everyone requires three payments; it is an established business practice.

Many subcontractors have requested three-part payments, so you sign the plumber's contract and give him the $6,000 deposit. The plumber says he can start the work in about two weeks. This is acceptable, and you agree to the anticipated start date. The plumber leaves with your deposit, and you are excited about your new bathrooms. Four or five days later, after your check has cleared, the plumber calls. He says you need to meet with him about some of your fixtures. When you ask if there is a problem, the plumber says it is nothing to worry about; he just needs to go over a few items.

The plumbing contractor arrives with your specifications sheet in hand. He explains that many of the fixtures you selected are special-order items, which require payment before the supplier will order them. This isn't too unusual; special orders often require full or partial payment in advance. The designer fixtures are expensive, and the contractor tells you the prepayment amount needed is $3,200. After assuring you the fixtures will be delivered in about three weeks, the contractor leaves, check in hand.

Time has passed and you are ready to have your rough plumbing installed. You call to schedule the contractor, and suddenly, the ever-present plumber doesn't return your phone calls. Even worse, you can't find the contractor anywhere. You have given this guy $9,200, and you have nothing except a signed contract. The address on the contract is a post-office box, and you have no idea what to do. At the worst, you have lost $9,200; at best, you have tied-up $9,200 in a court battle. If this sounds like a worst-case scenario, we will look at another outcome.

You call the plumber to do the rough-in, and he shows up as promised. By the end of the week, all your plumbing is roughed in. The plumber explains that he will come back and set your special-order whirlpool tub as soon as it is delivered. The code enforcement officer inspects and approves the work. Now the rough-in payment is due. The amount is one-third of the contract amount, or $6,000. The plumber explains that you already paid $1,800 of this amount by prepaying for the whirlpool. This reduces the rough-in payment to $4,200. You make the payment and get your lien waiver signed. The plumber says he will be back as soon as the whirlpool comes in.

Time passes. The plumber doesn't come back. Certainly the whirlpool must have been delivered by now. You start calling, but the phone is always answered by a machine. No one returns your calls. Now, let's do a little accounting. You paid the plumber a deposit of $6,000. Then you paid $3,200 for the special-order fixtures. Next you paid the rough-in draw of $4,200. The total contract amount is $18,000. So far you have paid $13,400 to the plumber. What do you have? You have about $1,000 worth of pipe and fittings installed and four days' labor for the plumber. You don't have any fixtures. At the most the work completed is worth $2,200. This means the plumber has recovered his cost and is enjoying the use of $11,200 of your money.

Maybe there is no intent to defraud you, or maybe there is. If a contractor sets up enough of these deals quickly, he could leave the state with a tidy sum. Sound farfetched? Some people are professionals at making a living by taking other people's money. Even if your contractor has every intention of fulfilling his contract, he has no reason to rush back to your job. When the contractor resumes work, he will have to spend the money you advanced and get your fixtures. His profit might amount to $3,600 when the job is complete. Right now, he has the use of over $11,000 of your money. Why should he hurry back? The plumber is able to call all the shots now. You are basically helpless. This is a position you don't want to be in.

Whoever has the money has the control. You can get in real trouble with a so-called standard payment schedule. The potential for problems exists with any trade, but the risks are greatest with the mechanical groups. Carpenters are on the job most of the time and are easier to keep track of. The mechanical trades can complete their rough-in work within a few days. Then they are gone until the job is nearly complete. When they are holding your money, too many problems can happen. The contractor could misappropriate the money, go out of business, or file for bankruptcy. When several different subcontractors are involved on your project, it is critical to manage your disbursements wisely.

> Never allow the contractor to gain control. You must set the pace.

ALTERNATIVE PAYMENT SCHEDULES

How can you protect yourself from this type of problem? Obviously, you must maintain financial control, but this is easier said than done. A payment schedule will have to be negotiated with every subcontractor when you act as your own general contractor. Hiring a general contractor requires only one negotiation; he has to dicker with the subs. If you convince the general to play by your rules, you have it made. Another way to reduce payment problems is to use a general contractor with "in-home" financing. Most of these plans don't deplete any of your existing cash with down payments or loan fees. Better yet, the contractors get one lump-sum payment when the job is finished to your satisfaction. This eliminates the three part payment risk altogether.

Whatever means you use, try to break the typical payment schedule. If a contractor wants the work badly enough, he will work with you on the terms. Perhaps he will accept a 15 percent deposit. This is a compromise for both of you. The contractor gets a deposit as a show of good faith on your part, and your position is stronger than it would be with a larger deposit.

Be honest with your contractors, but express your concerns in a way that won't offend them. A seasoned contractor will understand your concern but may not be willing to alter his payment schedule. Established contractors will have been stuck for payment more than once. This is like the proverbial "Mexican stand-off." The contractor doesn't trust the homeowner, and the homeowner doesn't trust the contractor. The difference is that the contractor has the built in protection of mechanic's liens. You have no protection. Work with your contractor to develop a satisfactory payment schedule. With a reasonable contractor you should be able to come to acceptable terms.

> Many contractors feel the need for a deposit to secure your job in their schedule. If they schedule materials and workers only to have you postpone or cancel the job, the contractors will lose money. They view the deposit as leverage to make sure you hold up your end of the agreement.

CODE COMPLIANCE AND JOB QUALITY

With a payment schedule agreed to, what are the other factors affecting the disbursements of payments? The most obvious is the completion of the prescribed work. Equally as important is the quality of the work. You should inspect all work closely before agreeing to release funds. In most cases, common sense and attention to detail are all you need to approve the quality of a job. Some things to look for include:

- Are the fixtures secure?
- Do doors open and close properly?
- Are there any unsightly lumps in the carpet or finished walls?
- Is the trim acceptable?
- Does everything work as it should?

These are the kinds of punch-list items to check. Many people assume the code enforcement officer will not approve the job unless everything is satisfactory. The code inspector's job is to ensure code compliance. He or she is not responsible for seeing that the job is done to your satisfaction. In some areas these inspectors do an outstanding job, but unfortunately this isn't always the case.

Often, small towns with limited budgets can't afford expert inspectors for each trade. They utilize one inspector for several trades. This can create problems. You can't expect a master electrician to know everything about the plumbing code. Neither can an expert carpenter be fully versed in heating systems. When you require a single inspector to be responsible for multiple trades, the potential for oversights increases.

High population areas have code officers for each trade, but they have to cover a larger number of inspections each day. Code officers may not have the time or ability to check for more than basic compliance. This means that you need to verify the quality of the work yourself.

Construction management consultants can be architects, independent consultants, or individual masters of each

If you aren't sure what to look for, consider hiring a construction management consultant. It might be to your advantage to hire a private, professional building inspector to check your work before you pay your contractor.

CONTRACTOR PUNCH LIST

Item/Phase	Okay	Repair	Replace	Finish Work

Notes:

COMMON PUNCH LIST

Phase	Okay	Needs Work

trade. Their services will not be cheap, but they can save you money in the long run. Their evaluation of the completed work will be unbiased and professional. These professional inspections can save you future frustration and problems. The expense should be between $50 and $100 per hour, which is a small price to pay for peace of mind. They will go over the workmanship with you, allowing you to question whether items should be accepted. When the work has been inspected and meets with your approval, advance the required payments. Remember to have lien waivers signed with each payment for services and materials.

There will be times when the work is not in compliance with the required codes. When this happens, notify the contractor in writing to correct the code violations. This can be done with the code violation notification form. Require the contractor to sign the form, acknowledging the work to be corrected. If you mail the form, do so by certified, return-receipt mail. It is vital to maintain a record of your notification and the contractor's acceptance of the mail regarding the code violations. This eliminates the contractor's ability to legitimately lien your property for nonpayment of the scheduled installment payment.

Keep accurate records and document all correspondence with your contractors. If you are forced into court, these records can win the case. Do not pay the contractor until all code violations are corrected. These violations can bring the progress of your job to a standstill. As we have discussed, each trade relies on another. When the plumber has to wait for a heating contractor to comply with a code violation, everyone, including you, loses time and money. For this reason, it is wise to have your contract stipulate a retainer on each payment.

Retainers are a safeguard against unknown problems and normally amount to 5 to 10 percent of the payment amount due. They are surrendered when the contractor complies with certain criteria. Final retainers should be withheld from each of your subcontractors for thirty days after completion of their work.

Your Company Name
Your Company Address
Your Company Phone and Fax Numbers

CODE VIOLATION NOTIFICATION

Contractor: _____

Contractor's address: _____

Contractor's city/state/zip: _____

Contractor's phone number: _____

Job location: _____

Date: _____

Type of work: _____

Subcontractor: _____

Address: _____

OFFICIAL NOTIFICATION OF CODE VIOLATIONS

On _____, 20 _____ , I was notified by the local code enforcement officer of code violations in the work performed by your company. The violations must be corrected within _____ (___) business days, as per our contract dated _____, 20 _____. Please contact the codes officer for a detailed explanation of the violations and required corrections. If the violations are not corrected within the allotted time, you may be penalized, as per our contract, for your actions in delaying the completion of this project. Thank you for your prompt attention to this matter.

_____   _____
General Contractor   Date

This allows for hidden or unforeseen problems to crop up. You cannot arbitrarily hold money due to the contractor, so include provisions in the contract allowing you to hold a retainer.

Keep tight reins on the contractors. Be fair, but don't put yourself in quicksand. Maintain strong financial leverage throughout the job. Money is a major motivator, and all contractors will respond to monetary motivation. A contract is good, but nothing is better for getting what you want than money.

Trying to enforce a contract is expensive and time-consuming. If you must prevail upon the courts to settle a dispute, even if you win the dispute, you lose. You lose time, money, and happiness. Good contracts and the right payment procedures keep you out of the judicial system.

You will have to make deposits and installment payments with most contractors. They consider this an accepted practice and many contractors will insist on it. If you refuse entirely, you may not be able to find contractors to do your work. With the exception of "in-home" financing, you will probably have to make deposits and payments to secure contractors. It is not unreasonable for a contractor to ask for deposits and progress payments. They are providing labor and materials with no guarantees of payment. This is a big risk, which can put a small contractor out of business.

Understand the contractor's position, and try to make him understand your concerns. Don't make demands. Negotiate with the contractor. There is always a way to work out amicable terms when both parties compromise. A well-defined, written payment plan benefits everyone. You will feel comfortable and remain in control, and the contractor will get paid on time. There will be no misunderstandings. Unless there is a breach of the agreement, there will be no need for a legal battle. This is good business for both you and the contractor.

Money accounts for most of the conflicts in remodeling. The initial argument may be started over material, but ultimately it is about money. Assume that you don't like the doors supplied by a contractor. There is more involved than your

Your Company Name
Your Company Address
Your Company Phone Number

REMODELING CONTRACT

This agreement, made this _____ day of _____, 20___, shall set forth the whole agreement, in its entirety, between Contractor and Customer.

Contractor: <u>Your Company Name</u>, referred to herein as Contractor.

Customer: _____, referred to herein as Customer.

Job name: _____

Job location: _____

The Customer and Contractor agree to the following:

SCOPE OF WORK

Contractor shall perform all work as described below and provide all material to complete the work described below. All work is to be completed by Contractor in accordance with the attached plans and specifications. All material is to be supplied by Contractor in accordance with the attached plans and specifications. Said attached plans and specifications have been acknowledged and signed by Contractor and Customer.

A brief outline of the work is as follows, and all work referenced in the attached plans and specifications will be completed to the Customer's reasonable satisfaction. The following is only a basic outline of the overall work to be performed: _____

_____
_____
_____
_____
_____
_____
_____
_____
_____

(Page 1 of 3. Please initial _____.)

COMMENCEMENT AND COMPLETION SCHEDULE

The work described above shall be started within _____ (_____) days of verbal notice from Customer; the projected start date is _____. The Contractor shall complete the above work in a professional and expedient manner, by no later than _____ (_____) days from the start date. Time is of the essence regarding this contract. No extension of time will be valid without the Customer's written consent. If Contractor does not complete the work in the time allowed, and if the lack of completion is not caused by the Customer, the Contractor will be charged _____ ($_____) dollars per day, for every day work is not finished beyond the completion date. This charge will be deducted from any payments due to the Contractor for work performed.

CONTRACT SUM

The Customer shall pay the Contractor for the performance of completed work, subject to additions and deductions, as authorized by this agreement or attached addendum. The contract sum is _____, ($_____).

PROGRESS PAYMENTS

The Customer shall pay the Contractor installments as detailed below, once an acceptable insurance certificate has been filed by the Contractor, with the Customer.

Customer will pay Contractor a deposit of _____
_____, ($_____), when work is started.

Customer will pay _____,
($_____), when all rough-in work is complete.

Customer will pay _____,
($_____) when work is _____ (_____%) percent complete.

Customer will pay _____,
($_____) when all work is complete and accepted.

All payments are subject to a site inspection and approval of work by the Customer. Before final payment, the Contractor, if required, shall submit satisfactory evidence to the Customer, that all expenses related to this work have been paid and no lien risk exists on the subject property.

WORKING CONDITIONS

Working hours will be _____ a.m. through _____ p.m., Monday through Friday. Contractor is required to clean work debris from the job site on a daily basis and to leave the site in a clean and neat condition. Contractor shall be responsible for removal and disposal of all debris related to the job description.

CONTRACT ASSIGNMENT

Contractor shall not assign this contract or subcontract the whole of this contract without the written consent of the Customer.

(Page 2 of 3. Please initial _____.)

LAWS, PERMITS, FEES, AND NOTICES

Contractor is responsible for all required laws, permits, fees, or notices required to perform the work stated herein.

WORK OF OTHERS

Contractor shall be responsible for any damage caused to existing conditions. This shall include work performed on the project by other contractors. If the Contractor damages existing conditions or work performed by other contractors, said Contractor shall be responsible for the repair of said damages. These repairs may be made by the Contractor responsible for the damages or another contractor, at the sole discretion of Customer.

The damaging Contractor shall have the opportunity to quote a price for the repairs. The Customer is under no obligation to engage the damaging Contractor to make the repairs. If a different contractor repairs the damage, the Contractor causing the damage may be back charged for the cost of the repairs. These charges may be deducted from any monies owed to the damaging Contractor.

If no money is owed to the damaging Contractor, said Contractor shall pay the invoiced amount within _____ (_____) business days. If prompt payment is not made, the Customer may exercise all legal means to collect the requested monies. The damaging Contractor shall have no rights to lien the Customer's property for money retained to cover the repair of damages caused by the Contractor. The Customer may have the repairs made to his or her satisfaction.

WARRANTY

Contractor warrants to the Customer all work and materials for one year from the final day of work performed.

INDEMNIFICATION

To the fullest extent allowed by law, the Customer shall indemnify and hold harmless the Contractor and all of his or her agents and employees from and against all claims, damages, losses, and expenses.

This Agreement entered into on _____, 20____ shall constitute the whole agreement between Customer and Contractor.

_____   _____
Customer   Date   Contractor   Date

_____
Customer   Date

(Page 3 of 3)

preference; you don't feel you should have to pay a premium price for unacceptable merchandise. Returning the doors will require someone's time and transportation. The contractor will be charged a restocking fee if he returns the doors. These problems cost the contractor money. Prices may have increased, and the replacement doors may be more expensive. The remodeler never planned on spending time or money changing doors. Everything involved in the change will cost the contractor money.

A dispute about doors is really about money. The doors are the focus of the problem, but money is basis of the problem. If you are willing to pay extra, the contractor would be glad to satisfy your requests. If not, this argument can grow into a serious conflict. You refuse to pay the contractor until you get the doors you want. The contractor refuses to work until he is paid for the work already completed. Something has to give. The contractor might file a lien and a lawsuit. You may try to sue the contractor. All of this will cost both of you more than the expense of changing the doors. By this time, the doors aren't the issue. Now you are both angry and defending your positions to the end.

This need to prevail hurts both of you. The contractor isn't getting paid, and your job isn't being completed. A weak contract probably caused the problem in the first place. Perhaps the doors weren't clearly specified. The next perpetrator was a vague payment clause. It called for payment in full when the doors were installed and was not contingent on your inspection and approval before disbursement. Now you have lost your leverage and are stuck with doors you don't want. By the letter of the contract and payment clause, the contractor is entitled to his money. You have a real problem and little chance of defending your position in court. The moral of the story is to insist on thorough, clear, written agreements. Make sure there is no room for error or questions in your contract and payment clauses. A contractor is likely to want you to sign a completion

Your Company Name
Your Company Address
Your Company Phone and Fax Numbers

CERTIFICATE OF COMPLETION AND ACCEPTANCE

Contractor: _____

Customer: _____

Job name: _____

Job location: _____

Job description: _____

_____

_____

_____

Date of completion: _____

Date of final inspection by customer: _____

Date of code compliance inspection and approval: _____

Defects found in material or workmanship: _____

_____

_____

_____

ACKNOWLEDGMENT

Customer acknowledges the completion of all contracted work and accepts all workmanship and materials as being satisfactory. Upon signing this certificate, the customer releases the contractor from any responsibility for additional work, except warranty work. Warranty work will be performed for a period of _____ from the date of completion. Warranty work will include the repair of any material or workmanship defects occurring between now and the end of the warranty period. All existing workmanship and materials are acceptable to the customer and payment will be made, in full, according to the payment schedule in the contract, between the two parties.

_____   _____
Customer   Date   Contractor   Date

certificate. Be sure that you are completely satisfied before signing such a document.

Keep all of your paperwork organized and available. You never know when you will need it, and this procedure will help safeguard you throughout your job and afterwards.

7

Putting It in Writing

Get it in writing! These four words convey the most important message in remodeling. The significance of having everything in writing cannot be stressed enough. Written documents solve problems before they happen and eliminate confusion. Concise written agreements protect your investment and assure your satisfaction. Without these agreements, you are exposed to a variety of uncontrollable, potentially devastating problems.

THE OUTLINE

The first form you will use is the outline. This form gives you the ability to document and organize your intended improvements in writing. No signatures or legal jargon are required in this form. It is simply an orderly list of your desires. A good outline should be arranged in chronological order. The categories create an overview of the scope of the work to be done. The information should focus on of the types of work you want

COST ESTIMATES FORM

Cost Projections For Bathroom Remodeling

Item/Phase	Labor	Material	Total
Plans			
Specifications			
Permits			
Trash container deposit			
Trash container delivery			
Demolition			
Dump fees			
Rough plumbing			
Rough electrical			
Rough heating/ac			
Subfloor			
Insulation			
Drywall			
Ceramic tile			
Linen closet			
Baseboard trim			
Window trim			
Door trim			
Paint/Wallpaper			
Underlayment			
Finish floor covering			
Linen closet shelves			

(continues)

done, not the products you intend to use. If you want to convert a closet or make room for a whirlpool tub, this is where you define the project. This outline will be helpful when you define your anticipated costs.

Keeping a written report of your remodeling interests will make your life simpler. You won't forget to price work in the

Item/Phase	Labor	Material	Total
Closet door & hardware			
Main door hardware			
Wall cabinets			
Base cabinets			
Counter tops			
Plumbing fixtures			
Trim plumbing material			
Final plumbing			
Shower enclosure			
Light fixtures			
Trim electrical material			
Final electrical			
Trim heating/ac material			
Final heating/ac			
Bathroom accessories			
Clean up			
Trash container removal			
Window treatments			
Personal touches			
Financing expenses			
Miscellaneous expenses			
Unexpected expenses			
Margin of error			
TOTAL ESTIMATED EXPENSE			

bidding stage, because the outline reminds you to request quotes. Put everything on the outline. Include the faucets you want replaced, the location of carpets to be installed, and the skylight you are considering. This is not a bid sheet, so put everything you want on it. You can edit the list later. It is only for proposed work.

CONTRACTOR SELECTION FORM

When your outline is complete, move on to the contractor selection form. This form is designed to aid during the contractor selection process. All the major groups of subcontractors are listed on the form, and you should note those you will need on your job. When you get to the bidding process, this list will be very helpful. Knowing which subs to call will be obvious, and omissions are less likely. The contractor selection form can also remind you of a phase of work previously forgotten.

You will know the types of contactors you may need to call, some of which could include:

- Carpenter
- Plumber
- Heating contractor
- Electrician
- Insulator
- Drywall contractor
- Painter
- Wallpaper contractor
- Flooring contractor

This form serves as a reminder of which trades will be needed to complete the work. You will need competitive bids for each phase of the job to plan your budget. A budget loses its effectiveness if you forget that you will need a tile contractor for your bathroom remodel. There are spaces on the form to list the name and phone number of the company you choose to do each phase of work. This allows you to use the form as a quick reference sheet during the project. The more you have in writing, the less you will forget.

CONTRACTOR QUESTIONNAIRE

PLEASE ANSWER ALL THE FOLLOWING QUESTIONS, AND EXPLAIN ANY "NO" ANSWERS.

Company name _____

Physical company address _____

Company mailing address _____

Company phone number _____

After hours phone number _____

Company President/Owner _____

President/Owner address _____

President/Owner phone number _____

How long has company been in business? _____

Name of insurance company _____

Insurance company phone number _____

Does company have liability insurance? _____

Amount of liability insurance coverage _____

Does company have Workman's Comp. insurance? _____

Type of work company is licensed to do _____

List Business or other license numbers _____

Where are licenses held? _____

If applicable, are all workman licensed? _____

Are there any lawsuits pending against the company? _____

Has the company ever been sued? _____

Does the company use subcontractors? _____

Is the company bonded? _____

Who is the company bonded with? _____

Has the company ever had complaints filed against it? _____

Are there any judgments against the company? _____

Please list 3 references of work similar to ours:

#1 _____

#2 _____

#3 _____

Please list 3 credit references:

#1 _____

#2 _____

#3 _____

Please list 3 trade references:

#1 _____

#2 _____

#3 _____

Please note any information you feel will influence our decision:

_____

ALL OF THE ABOVE INFORMATION IS TRUE AND ACCURATE AS OF THIS DATE.

DATE:_____ COMPANY NAME: _____

BY:_____ TITLE: _____

CONTRACTOR RATING SHEET

Job name: _____   Date: _____

Category	Contractor 1	Contractor 2	Contractor 3
Contractor name			
Returns calls			
Licensed			
Insured			
Bonded			
References			
Price			
Experience			
Years in business			
Work quality			
Availability			
Deposit required			
Detailed quote			
Personality			
Punctual			
Gut reaction			

Notes: _____

_____

_____

_____

_____

_____

CONTRACTOR COMPARISON SHEET

Category	Contractor 1	Contractor 2	Contractor 3
CONTRACTOR NAME			
RETURNS CALLS			
LICENSED			
INSURED			
BONDED			
REFERENCES			
PRICE			
EXPERIENCE			
YEARS IN BUSINESS			
WORK QUALITY			
AVAILABILITY			
DEPOSIT REQUIRED			
DETAILED QUOTE			
PERSONALITY			
PUNCTUAL			
GUT REACTION			

Notes: _____

_____

_____

_____

_____

_____

CONTRACTOR SELECTION FORM

TYPE OF SERVICE	VENDOR NAME	PHONE NUMBER	DATE SCHEDULED
Site Work	N/A		
Footings	N/A		
Concrete	N/A		
Foundation	N/A		
Waterproofing	N/A		
Masonry	N/A		
Framing	J. P. Buildal	231-8294	7/3/04
Roofing	N/A		
Siding	N/A		
Exterior Trim	N/A		
Gutters	N/A		
Pest Control	N/A		
Plumbing/R-I	TMG Plumbing, Inc.	242-1987	7/9/04
HVAC/R-I	Warming's HVAC	379-9071	7/15/04
Electrical/R-I	Bright Electric	257-2225	7/18/04
Central Vacuum	N/A		
Insulation	Allstar Insulators	242-4792	7/24/04
Drywall	Hank's Drywall	379-6638	7/29/04
Painter	J. C. Brush	247-8931	8/15/04
Wallpaper	N/A		
Tile	N/A		
Cabinets	N/A		
Countertops	N/A		
Interior Trim	The Final Touch Co.	365-1962	8/8/04
Floor Covering	Carpet Magicians	483-8724	8/19/04
Plumbing/Final	Same	Same	8/21/04
HVAC/Final	Same	Same	8/22/04
Electrical/Final	Same	Same	8/23/04
Cleaning	N/A		
Paving	N/A		
Landscaping	N/A		

NOTES/CHANGES _____

PROFESSIONAL SERVICES DIRECTORY

Now that you know the work you want done and the type of contractors you need to complete the job, the next document to use is the professional services directory. This form is similar to the contractor guide in that it lists all the services you will require. Use this form to reduce the risk of forgetting professionals who may be needed and who may not be at the top of your thoughts. Some examples of these types of professionals may include:

- Surveyors

- Architects

- Drafters

- Attorneys

- Insurance agency

- Home inspector

PROFESSIONAL SERVICES DIRECTORY

TYPE OF SERVICE	VENDOR NAME	PHONE NUMBER	DATE SCHEDULED
Survey	All-Pro Surveyors	555-9976	6/3/04
Attorney	B. C. Warden, Esq.	555-1738	6/5/04
Financing	Home Loans, Inc.	555-0080	6/27/04
Blueprints	Design Options, LTD.	555-2589	6/11/04
Accounting	A. G. Marks, CPA	555-3756	6/6/04
Appraisal	Valuall Appraisers	555-1789	6/12/04
Insurance	Quick-Claims Mutual	555-7898	7/2/04

QUERY LETTER

Your next written tool will be the Query Letter, which requests prices and inquires about the availability of services. Mailing this form letter to all the professionals you anticipate needing will save you time and money. The letter saves hours of phone calls to answering services.

> Mailed requests for information are an effective way to cover all the bases. You can send a letter to every contractor in the phone book and eliminate days of phone calls.

> Form letters allow you to achieve maximum results with minimal effort. They are effective with professionals, contractors, and suppliers alike. Written requests for service rates, material prices, and availability will eliminate disinterested parties. A form letter saves you untold time in wasted phone calls. Companies that respond to your letter will be eager for your business. These companies offer the best opportunity for good service and low prices.

PRODUCT INFORMATION SHEET

The next form you will need is the product identification sheet. This sheet is divided into construction phases. It will detail all the specifics of the products you are interested in. The sheet lists information such as:

- Brand name
- Model number
- Color
- Size
- Other pertinent information

> Don't allow substitutions without your written consent in the form of a change order.

Do you feel like you are being buried in paperwork? These forms don't have to be used, but the results without them are unpredictable at best. At this point you know the work you want done and the people required to do it. You even have your product list ready for bids. Are you ready to start the job? No, there is still work to be done in the office before the fieldwork is started.

ESTIMATED COST SHEET

Review the information you have assembled. Create files for all the suppliers and contractors. These files will help you during your negotiations and final decision. Using an estimated cost sheet is the next logical approach. This worksheet will give you a rough idea of the costs required to complete your remodeling project. The estimate sheet will be divided into phases of work, such as:

- Framing

- Siding

- Trim

- Electrical

- HVAC

- Plumbing

> Soft costs can add up to a staggering figure, so don't overlook them.

These phases are considered hard costs. In addition, your estimated cost sheet should include soft costs. These are professional fees, loan application fees, interest charges, and other broad-based costs.

The estimated cost sheet should include all expenses. You have to know what the total cash requirements will be before committing to a project. If you forget to include soft costs, you could run out of money before the job is finished. Review the sample cost sheets and add categories as needed. Some hidden expenses could be related to a home- improvement loan. These loans can require points, title searches, application fees, closing costs, and other financial expenses. Be aware of these potential costs and allow for them in your estimate.

FINE-TUNING THE PRELIMINARY DESIGN

With your estimating done, you can move on to the next step. This involves fine- tuning your preliminary design. Refer to the specifications sheet you have created. It should detail all the proposed materials for the job. It is time to begin to cross-reference the information in the stack of paperwork you have generated. The specifications sheet should be accompanied by a revised contractor list. Perhaps you found that you cannot afford a stone fireplace or quarry tile floor. These changes need to be reflected in your spec sheet. Adjust the estimated remodeling costs in accordance with your proposed changes. At this stage you are getting ready to get final quotes.

The changes you make within the specifications sheet may affect your contractor selection list. Changing the scope of the work may eliminate the need for some subcontractors. Make these notations on your contractor selection form. Don't waste time contacting contractors you don't need.

Every job should start with good written agreements and a strong production plan. Predicting an accurate financial budget is vital to completing a successful job.

BID REQUEST FORM

The bidding process is the financial backbone of your job. A Bid Request Form is an intricate part of the bidding process. Without it, you are dealing with ambiguous, bulk numbers.

CONTRACTOR QUESTIONNAIRE

When you are ready to start making commitments, you need to tie down the details. A contractor questionnaire can help with this important procedure. Some questions to ask potential contractors include:

- Do the contractors you plan to use have liability insurance?

- Do they provide worker's compensation insurance for their employees?

- Are their workers properly licensed?

- Does the contractor have the required business licenses?

- Is the contractor licensed to do the work you are requesting?

- Will the work performed be done by employees or subcontractors?

- Is the contractor bonded?

- Have the contractors and subcontractors ever had complaints filed against them by other customers?

These are questions you should answer before signing a contract. The questionnaire is designed to ask these questions without embarrassing you. When a contractor is asked to complete a form, they know you are requesting the same information from other contractors. This competition will provide the motivation for the contractor to answer the questions. The form also gives you the opportunity to get a contractor's answers in writing.

> It is easy for a remodeler to side-step your verbal questions or even to answer the questions with lies. Questionable contractors will think twice before answering with lies in writing; they could be charged with fraud. This is a proven way to cull the crop of bad contractors. Don't feel bad about asking them to complete this form. If they are good contractors, they will have no problem answering the questions in writing. The bad ones will disappear and save you a lot of trouble.

CONTRACTS

Once you find the right contractors, you are ready to proceed with your contracts. There is no reason to limit written contracts to tradespeople. While it not a routine business practice to contract with suppliers, it is a good idea. You can achieve additional assurances of your prices and delivery dates with a solid contract. Don't be afraid to ask for a contract from everyone involved in the project. Everything you have in writing reduces your risks.

A written contract with your general contractor or subcontractors is absolutely necessary. Contracts are an accepted requirement in building and remodeling. The contract should be strict but fair.

If you slant a contract too heavily to your advantage, contractors will not sign it. Most contractors will want you to sign their proposal or contract. They will have pre-printed forms, with the information regarding your job filled in the blank spaces. Contracts ultimately protect those who write them, so try to avoid using a contract supplied by others. Contractors may resist at first, but they will sign your contract if it's fair.

Legal documents such as contracts should be prepared by attorneys. Attorneys have the skill and knowledge to write contracts capable of standing the test of the courts.

A written contract is the last word in your job. It answers all the questions and calls all the shots. The contract is for your benefit, and you should have some input in its structure. Don't leave the contract preparation in the hands of a lawyer without providing your personal input. Lawyers know law, but they don't necessarily know remodeling or your needs and desires.

And, if you encounter a contractor who is in breech of contract, serve formal notice of the breech.

Now it's done; you have all your contracts signed. You probably thought you would never see the end of the paperwork. Well, you haven't; the job is only about to begin. There are reams of paper yet to be used. A successful job runs on paper. Without it you will suffer in the end. What else could you possibly need to put in writing? Some suggestions include, change orders, lien waivers, and completion certificates.

CHANGE ORDER

Once the job is started, it is sure to produce unexpected results. When these problems arise, you need to adapt your plans and agreements to accommodate any necessary changes. Use a written change order for every deviation from the contract. You must maintain consistency in your construc-

SAMPLE SUBCONTRACTOR-SUPPLIED CONTRACT

Anytime Plumbing & Heating
126 OCEAN STREET
BEACHTOWN, ME 00390
(000) 123-4567

PROPOSAL CONTRACT

TO: Mr. and Mrs. Homeowner   Date: 8/17/04
ADDRESS: 52 Your street Beachtown, ME 0039   PHONE: (000) 123-9876
JOB LOCATION: Same   JOB PHONE: Same   PLANS: Drawn by ACS, 4/14/04

ANYTIME PLUMBING & HEATING PROPOSES THE FOLLOWING:

Anytime Plumbing & Heating will supply and or coordinate all labor and material for the work referenced below:
PLUMBING

Supply and install a 3/4", type "L", copper water main from ten feet outside the foundation, to the location shown on the attached plans for the new addition.

Supply and install a 4", schedule 40, sewer main to the addition, from ten feet outside the foundation, to the location shown on the plans.

Supply and install schedule 40, steel gas pipe from the meter location, shown on the plans, to the furnace, in the attic, as shown on the plans.

Supply and install the following fixtures, as per plans, except as noted:
1 ABC Venus one piece, fiberglass, tub/shower unit, in white.
1 CF 007_222218 chrome tub/shower faucet.
1 ABC 900928 water closet combination, in white.
1 CBA 111 cultured marble, 30" vanity top, in white.
1 CF 005-95011 chrome lavatory faucet.
1 PKT 11122012 stainless steel, double bowl, kitchen sink.
1 CF 908001 chrome kitchen faucet.
1 DFG 62789 52 gallon, electric, 5 year warranty, water heater.
1 WTFC 20384 frost proof, anti-siphon silcock.
1 AWD 90576 3/4" backflow preventer.
1 FT66754W white, round front, water closet seat.
1 plastic washer box, with hose bibs.
Connect owner supplied dishwasher.

All fixtures are subject to substitution with fixtures of similar quality, at Anytime Plumbing & Heating's discretion.

All water distribution pipe, after the water meter, will be Pex tubing, run under the slab. This is a change from the specifications and plans, in an attempt to reduce cost.

(Page 1 of 3) Initials_____

SAMPLE SUBCONTRACTOR-SUPPLIED CONTRACT (continued)

If water pipe is run as specified in the plans, the pipe will be, type "L" copper and there will be additional cost. Any additional cost will be added to the price listed in this proposal.

All waste and vent pipes will be schedule 40 PVC.

Anytime Plumbing & Heating will provide for trenching the inside of the foundation, for underground plumbing. If the trenching is complicated by rock, unusual depth, or other unknown factors, there will be additional charges. These charges will be for the extra work involved in the trenching.

All plumbing will be installed to comply with state and local codes. Plumbing installation may vary from the plumbing diagrams drawn on the plans.

Anytime Plumbing & Heating will provide roof flashings for all pipes penetrating the roof, but will not be responsible for their installation.

All required holes in the foundation will be provided by others.

All trenching, outside of the foundation, will be provided by others.

All gas piping, outside the structure, will be provided by others.

The price for this plumbing work will be, Four Thousand, Eighty Seven Dollars ($4,087.00).

HEATING

Anytime Plumbing & Heating will supply and install all duct work and registers, as per plans.

Anytime Plumbing & Heating will supply and install a BTDY-P5HSD12NO7501 gas fired, forced hot air furnace. The installation will be, as per plans. The homeowner will provide adequate access for this installation.

Venting for the clothes dryer and exhaust fan is not included in this price. The venting will be done at additional charge, if requested.

No air conditioning work is included.

The price for the heating work will be Three Thousand, Eight Hundred Dollars ($3,800.00).

Any alterations to this contract will only be valid, if in writing and signed by all parties. Verbal arrangements will not be binding.

PAYMENT WILL BE AS FOLLOWS:

Contract Price of: Seven Thousand, Eight Hundred Eighty-Seven Dollars ($7,887.00), to be paid; one third ($2,629.00) at the signing of the contract. One third ($2,627.00) when the plumbing and heating is roughed-in. One third ($2,629.00) when work is completed. All payments shall be made within five business days of the invoice date.

(Page 2 of 3) Initials_____

SAMPLE SUBCONTRACTOR-SUPPLIED CONTRACT (continued)

If payment is not made according to the terms above, Anytime Plumbing & Heating will have the following rights and remedies. Anytime Plumbing & Heating may charge a monthly service charge of one percent (1%), twelve percent (12%) per year, from the first day default is made. Anytime Plumbing & Heating may lien the property where the work has been done. Anytime Plumbing & Heating may use all legal methods in the collection of monies owed to Anytime Plumbing & Heating. Anytime Plumbing & Heating may seek compensation, at the rate of $50.00 per hour, for their employees attempting to collect unpaid monies. Anytime Plumbing & Heating may seek payment for legal fees and other costs of collection, to the full extent that law allows.

If Anytime Plumbing & Heating is requested to send men or material to a job by their customer or their customer's representative, the following policy shall apply. If a job is not ready for the service or material requested, and the delay is not due to Anytime Plumbing & Heating's actions, Anytime Plumbing & Heating may charge the customer for their efforts in complying with the customer's request. This charge will be at a rate of $50.00 per hour, per man, including travel time.

If you have any questions or don't understand this proposal, seek professional advice. Upon acceptance this becomes a binding contract between both parties.

Respectfully submitted,

H. P. Contractor
Owner

PROPOSAL EXPIRES IN 30 DAYS, IF NOT ACCEPTED BY ALL PARTIES

ACCEPTANCE
We the undersigned, do hereby agree to and accept all the terms and conditions of this proposal. We fully understand the terms and conditions and hereby consent to enter into this contract.

Anytime Plumbing & Heating   Customer #1
by_____   _____
Title_____   Date_____

Date_____   Customer #2
                                    _____
                                    Date_____

(Page 3 of 3)

Your Company Name
Your Company Address
Your Company Phone and Fax Numbers

SUBCONTRACTOR AGREEMENT

This agreement, made this _____ day of _____, 20__, shall set forth the whole agreement, in its entirety, between Contractor and Subcontractor.

Contractor: _____, referred to herein as Contractor.

Job location: _____

Subcontractor: _____, referred to herein as Subcontractor.

The Contractor and Subcontractor agree to the following.

SCOPE OF WORK

Subcontractor shall perform all work as described below and provide all material to complete the work described below.

Subcontractor shall supply all labor and material to complete the work according to the attached plans and specifications. These attached plans and specifications have been initialed and signed by all parties. The work shall include, but is not limited to, the following: _____
_____
_____
_____
_____

COMMENCEMENT AND COMPLETION SCHEDULE

The work described above shall be started within _____ (___) days of verbal notice from Contractor, the projected start date is _____. The Subcontractor shall complete the above work in a professional and expedient manner by no later than _____ (___) days from the start date. Time is of the essence in this contract. No extension of time will be valid without the Contractor's written consent. If Subcontractor does not complete the work in the time allowed, and if the lack of completion is not caused by the Contractor, the Subcontractor will be charged _____ ($_____) dollars per day, for every day work extends beyond the completion date. This charge will be deducted from any payments due to the Subcontractor for work performed.

(Page 1 of 3. Please initial _____.)

SUBCONTRACTOR AGREEMENT (continued)

CONTRACT SUM

The Contractor shall pay the Subcontractor for the performance of completed work subject to additions and deductions as authorized by this agreement or attached addendum. The contract sum is

_____($_____).

PROGRESS PAYMENTS

The Contractor shall pay the Subcontractor installments as detailed below, once an acceptable insurance certificate has been filed by the Subcontractor with the Contractor. Contractor shall pay the Subcontractor as described: _____

   All payments are subject to a site inspection and approval of work by the Contractor. Before final payment, the Subcontractor shall submit satisfactory evidence to the Contractor that no lien risk exists on the subject property.

WORKING CONDITIONS

Working hours will be _____ a.m. through _____ p.m., Monday through Friday. Subcontractor is required to clean work debris from the job site on a daily basis and leave the site in a clean and neat condition. Subcontractor shall be responsible for removal and disposal of all debris related to the job description.

CONTRACT ASSIGNMENT

Subcontractor shall not assign this contract or further subcontract the whole of this subcontract, without the written consent of the Contractor.

LAWS, PERMITS, FEES, AND NOTICES

Subcontractor shall be responsible for all required laws, permits, fees, or notices, required to perform the work stated herein.

WORK OF OTHERS

Subcontractor shall be responsible for any damage caused to existing conditions or other contractor's work. This damage will be repaired, and the Subcontractor charged for the expense and supervision of this work. The Subcontractor shall have the opportunity to quote a price for said repairs, but the Contractor is under no obligation to engage the Subcontractor to make said repairs. If a different subcontractor repairs the damage, the Subcontractor may be back charged for the cost of the repairs. Any repair costs will be deducted from any payments due to the Subcontractor. If no payments are due the Subcontractor, the Subcontractor shall pay the invoiced amount within _____ (____) days.

(Page 2 of 3. Please initial _____.)

SUBCONTRACTOR AGREEMENT (continued)

WARRANTY

Subcontractor warrants to the Contractor, all work and materials for
_____ from the final day of work performed.

INDEMNIFICATION

To the fullest extent allowed by law, the Subcontractor shall indemnify and
hold harmless the Owner, the Contractor, and all of their agents and
employees from and against all claims, damages, losses, and expenses.

This agreement, entered into on _____, 20_____, shall
constitute the whole agreement between Contractor and Subcontractor.

_____   _____
Contractor   Date   Subcontractor   Date

(Page 3 of 3)

Your Company Name
Your Company Address
Your Company Phone and Fax Numbers

SUBCONTRACTOR CONTRACT ADDENDUM

This addendum is an integral part of the contract dated
_____, between the Contractor, _____,
and the Customer(s), _____, for
the work being done on real estate commonly known as _____.

The undersigned parties hereby agree to the following:

_____
_____
_____
_____

The above constitutes the only additions to the above-mentioned contract.
No verbal agreements or other changes shall be valid unless made in
writing and signed by all parties.

_____   _____
Contractor   Date   Customer   Date

                                          _____
                                          Customer   Date

Your Company Name
Your Company Address
Your Company Phone and Fax Numbers

NOTICE OF BREACH OF CONTRACT

Date: _____

To: _____   From: _____

_____   _____

_____   _____

TAKE NOTICE that under Contract made _____, 20 _____, as evidenced by the following documents: _____, we are hereby holding you IN BREACH for the following reasons: _____

_____

_____

_____

   If your Breach is not cured within _____ days (i.e., cure must be completed by _____, 20 _____), we will take all further actions necessary to mitigate our damages and protect our rights, which may include, but are not necessarily limited to, the right to Cover" by obtaining substitute performance and chargeback to you of all additional costs and damages incurred.

   This Notice is made under the Uniform Commercial Code (if applicable) and all other applicable laws. All rights are hereby reserved, none of which are waived. Any forbearance or temporary waiver from enforcement shall not constitute permanent waiver or waiver of any other right.

   You are urged to cure your Breach forthwith.

_____

Contractor

By: _____
     Authorized Signatory

tion management. Written change orders reinforce your dedication to have every aspect of the work clearly defined in black and white.

During the job, you will be tempted to avoid all of this paperwork, especially change orders. You will gain a comfort level with your contractors, which will make change orders seem unnecessary. If you get a phone call at the office regarding mandatory alterations, you will be tempted to give verbal authorization for changes over the phone. Resist these urges. If the situation demands immediate verbal authorization, follow it up with a change order as soon as possible. It is important to maintain continuity. If you start making exceptions, your paperwork will become almost useless.

Contractors will be less likely to take advantage of you when change orders are used, and there will be fewer misunderstandings. Requiring the use of written change orders prevents unexpected price increases. Your contract should mention that change orders will be required for any changes or additional work. In this way a contractor is not entitled to payment for extra work unless you first authorize it in writing. By requiring written change orders, you will be better prepared if you find yourself in court.

CODE COMPLIANCE FORMS

As work progresses, contractors will want to be paid. In most cases, local code- enforcement inspections will be required on the work done. Don't advance any payments until these inspections are completed and accepted. The codes office will provide written evidence of satisfactory inspections. Insist on a copy of each inspection certificate from the contractor. This protects you from code-violation problems. If a code officer turns down an inspection, complete a code violation notification and give it to the appropriate contractor. This notification

Going to court is never a planned part of remodeling. It is an activity you want to avoid. The best way to bypass the courts is to maintain clear, concise, written agreements.

Your Company Name
Your Company Address
Your Company Phone and Fax Number

CHANGE ORDER

This change order is an integral part of the contract dated_____,
between the customer _____, and the contractor,
_____, for the work to be
performed. The job location is _____. The following changes are
the only changes to be made. These changes shall now become a part of
the original contract and may not be altered again without written
authorization from all parties.
Changes to be as follows:

_____
_____
_____
_____
_____

These changes will increase / decrease the original contract amount.
Payment for theses changes will be made as follows:
_____. The amount of
change in the contract price will be
_____ ($_____). The new total
contract price shall be _____
($_____).

The undersigned parties hereby agree that these are the only changes to
be made to the original contract. No verbal agreements will be valid. No
further alterations will be allowed without additional written authorization,
signed by all parties. This change order constitutes the entire agreement
between the parties to alter the original contract.

_____   _____
Customer   Contractor

_____   _____
Date   Date

_____
Customer

_____
Date

CODE VIOLATION NOTIFICATION

CUSTOMER NAME: Mr. & Mrs. J. P. Homeowner
CUSTOMER ADDRESS: 192 Hometown Street
CUSTOMER CITY/STATE/ZIP: Ourtown, MO 00580
CUSTOMER PHONE NUMBER: (000) 555-1212
JOB LOCATION: Same
DATE: July 25, 2004
TYPE OF WORK: Electrical
CONTRACTOR: Flashy Electrical Service
ADDRESS: 689 Walnut Ridge, Boltz, MO 00580

OFFICIAL NOTIFICATION OF CODE VIOLATIONS

On July 24, 2004, I was notified by the local electrical code enforcement officer of code violations in the work performed by your company. The violations must be corrected within two business days, as per our contract dated July 1, 2004. Please contact the codes officer for a detailed explanation of the violations and required corrections. If the violations are not corrected within the allotted time, you may be penalized, as per our contract, for your actions, delaying the completion of this project. Thank you for your prompt attention to this matter.

_____   _____

J. P. Homeowner   Date

gives the contractor a specific period of time to have the work corrected and approved by the code officer. In this way you avoid delays, which may affect other trades and throw your project way off schedule. Stipulate in the contract your desire for a photocopy of all permits and inspection results.

LIEN WAVER FORM

Before paying anyone, you should complete a lien waiver form. One of these should be signed by any vendor receiving money for services or materials related to your job. Require the lien waiver to be signed at the time you make payment for the service or material. The lien waiver is like your receipt for issuing payment and will protect your home from mechanic's and materialman's liens.

> Never advance money to a contractor until the work passes the inspection of the local code officer.

PUNCH LIST

A punch list is a written notice to contractors of items left to be completed or repaired. These lists come into play at the end of the job. When contractors are finished, you should inspect all the work before final payment is made. Use the punch list form to note all unsatisfactory or incomplete workmanship or materials. After your inspection and before final payment, present a copy of the punch list to the contractor. Have the contractor agree to the list by signing it and allow a reasonable time for corrections to be made. When the punch work is done, inspect the job again. If there are still deficiencies, complete another punch list. Continue this process until the work is done to your satisfaction.

Here is some advice about the proper usage of the punch list:

- Remember that, throughout the remodeling process, we have stressed the need to be fair.

PUNCH LIST

BATHROOM REMODELING PROJECT

ITEM/PHASE	O.K.	REPAIR	REPLACE	FINISH WORK
Demolition				
Rough plumbing				
Rough electrical				
Rough heating/ac				
Subfloor				
Insulation				
Drywall				
Ceramic tile				
Linen closet				
Baseboard trim				
Window trim				
Door trim				
Paint/Wallpaper				
Underlayment				
Finish floor covering				
Linen closet shelves				
Linen closet door				
Closet door hardware				
Main door hardware				
Wall cabinets				
Base cabinets				
Countertops				
Plumbing fixtures				
Trim plumbing material				
Final plumbing				
Shower enclosure				
Light fixtures				
Trim electrical material				
Final electrical				
Trim heating/ac material				
Final heating/ac				
Bathroom accessories				
Clean up				

NOTES _____

_____

_____

- Be realistic about the work you demand on the punch list.

- Don't require the contractor to replace an entire roll of wallpaper just because there is a tiny wrinkle down by the floor.

- Do not allow a contractor to bully you into accepting work with obvious or offensive flaws.

- Be very thorough when you make the first punch list. Contractors will be quickly angered if they repair everything on your list only to have you find additional items that you missed in your initial inspection.

- Only add items to the list that were caused by the punch work.

You can use a retainer system when dealing with a punch list. Your contractor will want some payment before doing the punch list, and this is okay. But make sure that you retain enough money to pay some other contractor if necessary to have the problems corrected.

CERTIFICATE OF COMPLETION

Certificates of completion document the conclusion dates of all work performed. This form is important in determining your warranty period. Contractors normally offer one-year warranties on their work, and the manufacturer's warranty applies to individual products. These warranties should start with the date on the completion certificate. These simple forms take the guesswork out of warranty claims. They clearly establish the date all work was completed, inspected, and approved. This little piece of paper can make a big difference if you have a major malfunction or problem.

Many of the problems in remodeling are not caused by intentional deceit; they are caused by confusion. You are thinking one thing, and the contractor is thinking something

SAMPLE CERTIFICATE OF COMPLETION AND ACCEPTANCE

CONTRACTOR: _Willy's Drywall Service_

CUSTOMER: _David R Erastus_

JOB NAME: _Erastus_

JOB LOCATION: _134 Faye Lane, Beau, VA 29999_

JOB DESCRIPTION: _Supply and install drywall in new addition, as per plans and specifications, and as described in the contract dated, 6/10/04, between the two parties. Hang, tape, sand, and prepare wall and ceiling surfaces for paint._

DATE OF COMPLETION: _August 13, 2004_

DATE OF FINAL INSPECTION BY CUSTOMER: _August 13, 2004_

DATE OF CODE COMPLIANCE INSPECTION & APPROVAL: _August 13, 2004_

ANY DEFICIENCIES FOUND BY CUSTOMER: _None_

NOTE ANY DEFECTS IN MATERIAL OR WORKMANSHIP: _None_

ACKNOWLEDGEMENT

Customer acknowledges the completion of all contracted work and accepts all workmanship and materials as being satisfactory. Upon signing this certificate, the customer releases the contractor from any responsibility for additional work, except warranty work. Warranty work will be performed for a period of one year from August 13, 2004. Warranty work will include the repair of any material or workmanship defects occurring after this date. All existing workmanship and materials are acceptable to the customer and payment will be made, in full, according to the payment schedule in the contract, between the two parties.

Customer	Date	Contractor	Date

SAMPLE DAMAGE CLAUSE

CONTRACTOR LIABILITY FOR DAMAGES TO EXISTING CONDITIONS

Contractor shall be responsible for any damage caused to existing conditions. This shall include work performed on the project by other contractors. If the contractor damages existing conditions or work performed by other contractors, said contractor shall be responsible for the repair of said damages. These repairs may be made by the contractor responsible for the damages or another contractor, at the discretion of the homeowner.

If a different contractor repairs the damage, the contractor causing the damage may be back-charged for the cost of the repairs. These charges may be deducted from any monies owed to the damaging contractor, by the homeowner. The choice for a contractor to repair the damages shall be at the sole discretion of the homeowner.

If no money is owed to the damaging contractor, said contractor shall pay the invoiced amount, from the homeowner, within seven business days. If prompt payment is not made, the homeowner may exercise all legal means to collect the requested monies.

The damaging contractor shall have no rights to lien the homeowner's property, for money retained to cover the repair of damages caused by the contractor. The homeowner may have the repairs made to their satisfaction.

The damaging contractor shall have the opportunity to quote a price for the repairs. The homeowner is under no obligation to engage the damaging contractor to make the repairs.

else. You both have good intentions, but the conflict can get out of hand. Neither of you will want to give ground in the dispute when money is involved. With oral agreements there is no way to determine who is right. Written agreements eliminate the source of confusion. Each party knows exactly what he or she is expected to do and what he or she will be getting from the contractual relationship. It is also a good idea to include a clause about any damage that a contractor may cause during a job. Many problems arise when contractors damage personal property or the work of others.

Working with close friends can be the worst experience of your life. Business is business, and it can become a true threat to relationships. Friends don't want to insult each other; consequently, they avoid written contracts. Trust is not a factor, and the lack of a good contract can ruin your friendship. Financial disputes can turn into an all-out battle. The friend you golf with every week can become your worst enemy over a simple misunderstanding. Written contracts protect you and your friends.

8

Keeping Your
Contractor Honest

Contractors have mixed reputations. Like any other profession, there are good ones and bad ones. As a consumer, you have to try to find the good ones. The process for finding contractors was explained earlier. Now we are going to examine ways to make sure these contractors give you what you want. The two most important elements in controlling a contractor are money and a firm contract. Some of the ways to maintain control have already been touched on. Here we are going to expand on the methods for commanding respect and maintaining control.

CONTRACTS

Control is established during your initial negotiations with contractors and suppliers. A comprehensive contract, which you supply, will cement your dominant position. Proposals supplied by contractors will not be slanted to benefit you. A good contract is critical to the success of any remodeling job.

Subcontractor agreements will differ with various trades. The basic language will remain the same, but some clauses will change. These clauses will be directly related to the type of work the subcontractor is supplying. The language required in a foundation contract will differ dramatically from that in a roofing proposal.

When you talk to a contractor, you may be creating a legal contract. Contracts don't have to be in writing to be lawful; verbal contracts are perfectly legal. The problem is implementing a verbal contract. If you only have an oral agreement, how will you enforce it? There will be nothing in writing to substantiate your claims. When a dispute occurs, it is your word against the contractor's. This can be an impossible situation to settle fairly. This is the difference between legal and enforceable. Talk to your attorney, and get the proper documents for the job. It is difficult for a contractor to argue with the terms of a written contract. In addition to the types of contracts that you have seen to this point, you will want to be sure that your contractors are independent contractors and will not be considered an employee of yours. Have your attorney draft documents to cover this type of contract, as well. Another type of contract that might be used for some professionals is a letter of engagement. Ask your lawyer if you should have this type of document on hand.

> When your contracts are prepared by a local attorney, you know they are legal and enforceable. A good contract must be both. There is a big difference between legal and enforceable.

> Don't settle for a vague or simplified form contract. Personalize the contract to meet the needs of your particular job.

The various components of a contract can be complex or simple. The main objective is to have every aspect of the job covered in writing. You don't need fancy legal terms; you only need a clear, concise description of the agreed-upon work and terms.

Your Company Name
Your Company Address
Your Company Phone and Fax Numbers

INDEPENDENT CONTRACTOR ACKNOWLEDGMENT

Undersigned hereby enters into a certain arrangement or affiliation with Your Company Name, as of this date. The Undersigned confirms:

1. Undersigned is an independent contractor and is not an employee, agent, partner or joint venturer of or with the Company.

2. Undersigned shall not be entitled to participate in any vacation, medical or other fringe benefit or retirement program of the Company and shall not make claim of entitlement to any such employee program or benefit.

3. Undersigned shall be solely responsible for the payment of withholding taxes, FICA and other such tax deductions on any earnings or payments made, and the Company shall withhold no such payroll tax deductions from any payments due. The Undersigned agrees to indemnify and reimburse the Company from any claim or assessment by any taxing authority arising from this paragraph.

4. Undersigned and Company acknowledge that the Undersigned shall not be subject to the provisions of any personnel policy or rules and regulations applicable to employees, as the Undersigned shall fulfill his/her responsibility independent of and without supervisory control by the Company.

Signed under seal this _____ day of _____ , 20___ .

_____   _____
Independent Contractor   Company Representative

                                    _____
                                    Title

Your Company Name
Your Company Address
Your Company Phone and Fax Numbers

INDEPENDENT CONTRACTOR AGREEMENT

I understand that as an Independent Contractor I am solely responsible for my health, actions, taxes, insurance, transportation, and any other responsibilities that may be involved with the work I will be doing as an Independent Contractor.

I will not hold anyone else responsible for any claims or liabilities that may arise from this work or from any cause related to this work. I waive any rights I have or may have to hold anyone liable for any reason as a result of this work.

_____

Independent Contractor   Date

_____

Witness   Date

Contract Details

One of the first sections of your contract should focus on the contractor's information. These details should include:

- The company name
- The names of principals in the company
- A physical address
- All available phone numbers

Your Company Name
Your Company Address
Your Company Phone and Fax Numbers

LETTER OF ENGAGEMENT

Client: _____

Street: _____

City/State/Zip: _____

Work phone: _____ Home phone: _____

Services requested: _____

_____

_____

Fee for services described above: $ _____

Payment to be made as follows: _____

_____

By signing this letter of engagement, you indicate your understanding that this engagement letter constitutes a contractual agreement between us for the services set forth. This engagement does not include any services not specifically stated in this letter. Additional services, which you may request, will be subject to separate arrangements, to be set forth in writing.

A representative of _____ has advised us that we should seek legal counsel prior to using information or materials received from _____

_____

We the undersigned hereby release _____, its employees, officers, shareholders, and representatives from any liability. We understand that we shall have no rights, claims, or recourse and waive any claims or rights we may have against _____, its employees, officers, shareholders, and representatives. We further understand that we will pay all costs of collection of any amount due hereunder including reasonable attorney's fees.

_____   _____
Client   Date   Client   Date

_____
Company Representative   Date

SAMPLE OWNER-SUPPLIED SUBCONTRACT AGREEMENT

RICHARD & RHONDA SMART
180 HOMEOWNER LANE
WIZETOWN, OH 99897
(102) 555-6789

SUBCONTRACT AGREEMENT

This agreement, made this 25th day of July, 2004, shall set forth the whole agreement, in its entirety, between Contractor and Subcontractor.

Contractor: Richard & Rhonda Smart, referred to herein as Contractor.
Job location: 180 Homeowner Lane, Wizetown, OH
Subcontractor: Wild Bill's Painting company, referred to herein as Subcontractor.

The Contractor and Subcontractor agree to the following:

SCOPE OF WORK

Subcontractor shall perform all work as described below and provide all material to complete the work described below:

Subcontractor shall supply all labor and material to complete the work according to the attached plans and specifications. These attached plans and specifications have been initialed and signed by all parties. The work shall include, but is not limited to, the following:

(1) Scrape all painted surfaces in the family room, living room, and bedrooms.
(2) Fill all cracks and holes with joint compound.
(3) Sand painted surfaces as needed and prepare all painted surfaces for new paint.
(4) Provide protection from paint or other substance spillage.
(5) Move and replace any obstacles, furniture, or other items in the area to be painted.
(6) Prime all surfaces to be painted with an approved primer.
(7) Paint all existing painted surfaces with two coats of a Latex paint, color number LT1689.
(8) Remove any excess paint from window glass or other areas not intended to be painted.
(9) Complete all work in strict compliance with the attached plans and specifications.

(Page 1 of 3 initials _____)

SAMPLE OWNER-SUPPLIED SUBCONTRACT (continued)

COMMENCEMENT AND COMPLETION SCHEDULE

The work described above shall be started within three days of verbal notice from Contractor, the projected start date is 8/20/04. The Subcontractor shall complete the above work in a professional and expedient manner by no later than twenty days from the start date. Time is of the essence in this Subcontract. No extension of time will be valid without the Contractor's written consent. If Subcontractor does not complete the work in the time allowed, and if the lack of completion is not caused by the Contractor, the Subcontractor will be charged Fifty Dollars ($50.00) per day, for every day work extends beyond the completion date. This charge will be deducted from any payments due to the Subcontractor for work performed.

CONTRACT SUM

The Contractor shall pay the Subcontractor for the performance of completed work, subject to additions and deductions, as authorized by this agreement or attached addendum. The Contract Sum is Two Thousand Dollars ($2,000.00).

PROGRESS PAYMENTS

The Contractor shall pay the Subcontractor installments as detailed below, once an acceptable insurance certificate has been filled by the Subcontractor with the Contractor:

Contractor shall pay the Subcontractor Five Hundred Dollars ($500.00), when materials are delivered and preparation work is started.

Contractor shall pay the Subcontractor Five Hundred Dollars ($500.00), when preparation work is complete and painting is started.

Contractor shall pay the Subcontractor Eight Hundred Dollars ($800.00), when all work is complete and approved by the Contractor.

Contractor shall pay the Subcontractor Two Hundred Dollars ($200.00), thirty days after completion and acceptance of work, if no deficiencies are found in materials or workmanship during the thirty day period.

All payments are subject to a site inspection and approval of work by the Contractor. Before final payment, the Subcontractor, shall submit satisfactory evidence to the Contractor that no lien risk exists on the subject property.

(Page 2 of 3 initials _____)

SAMPLE OWNER-SUPPLIED SUBCONTRACT (continued)

WORKING CONDITIONS

Working hours will be 8:00 a.m. through 4:30 a.m., Monday through Friday. Subcontractor is required to clean his work debris from the job site on a daily basis and leave the site in a clean and neat condition. Subcontractor shall be responsible for removal & disposal of all debris related to his job description.

CONTRACT ASSIGNMENT

Subcontractor shall not assign this contract or further subcontract the whole of this subcontract, without the written consent of the Contractor.

LAWS, PERMITS, FEES, AND NOTICES

Subcontractor shall be responsible for all required laws, permits, fees, or notices, required to perform the work stated herein.

WORK OF OTHERS

Subcontractor shall be responsible for any damage caused to existing conditions or other contractor's work. This damage will be repaired, and the Subcontractor charged for the expense and supervision of this work. The Subcontractor shall have the opportunity to quote a price for said repairs, but the Contractor is under no obligation to engage the Subcontractor to make said repairs. If a different subcontractor repairs the damage, the Subcontractor may be back-charged for the cost of the repairs.

Any repair costs will be deducted from any payments due to the Subcontractor, if any exist. If no payments are due the Subcontractor, the Subcontractor shall pay the invoiced amount within ten days.

WARRANTY

Subcontractor warrants to the Contractor, all work and materials for one year from the final day of work performed.

INDEMNIFICATION

To the fullest extent allowed by law, the Subcontractor shall indemnify and hold harmless the Owner, the Contractor, and all of their agents and employees from and against all claims, damages, losses and expenses. This agreement, entered into on July 25, 2004, shall constitute the whole agreement between Contractor and Subcontractor.

Contractor	Subcontractor
Richard B. Smart	Rhonda M. Smart
	(Page 3 of 3 initials _____)

In this phase of the remodeling adventure, the more information you have, the better your chances are of obtaining what you want. Contractors with bad intentions will not be cooperative with information. They don't want you to be able to find them. They will try to hide behind answering machines and post-office boxes to reduce your ability to make personal contact. Requesting extensive information will reduce the chances of a bad experience.

The next important element will be an accurate description of the job location. You should use the street or legal address of your job in the contract. A street address is sufficient, but a legal description removes any doubt. Legal descriptions include:

> Don't accept a post-office box for an address. Insist on a physical location for the business. This will be beneficial if you have to serve the company with legal papers. Get as many phone numbers as you can, including home phones and home addresses. A contractor may not want you to bother him at home, but if you can obtain this information, you are ahead of the game.

- The lot number

- The block number

- The tax-map section of the property

- In some areas, a legal description will be the same as a deed description

- Deeds frequently summarize property in the metes and bounds format

Regardless of the language, your attorney will know what type of legal description to use. A detailed location for the work to be completed is extremely important.

There have been occasions when work was performed on the wrong house. One such instance involved the resurfacing of a gravel driveway. A customer called a stone company and requested several loads of stone to be added to their existing driveway. The company agreed to bill the customer for the work and asked for the delivery address. The customer gave the address and directions. The work was scheduled for later in the week. The homeowner said he wouldn't be home, but the driver could drop off the stone and leave the bill in the front door. This was acceptable to the company, and the work was scheduled.

The day for the delivery arrived. When the customer returned from work, he was surprised not to find any stone in his driveway. It was late, and the stone company had already closed for the day, so the customer called the company the next morning. When the customer asked the owner of the company why his stone had not been delivered, the owner insisted it had been delivered. He checked his driver's tickets from the previous day, and confirmed the delivery had been made. Obviously, this was confusing for both parties. The owner of the company agreed to investigate the situation and call the customer back.

The owner then received another phone call from one of his good friends. His friend said a mistake had been made. He went on to explain that he had come home and found new gravel in his driveway. There was also a delivery ticket in his front door, but the ticket was made out to a customer in another part of town. The street number on the ticket was correct, but the street name was wrong. The delivery had been made to South Street, but was intended for South Circle.

One simple word was responsible for a potentially large problem. The friend who received the stone had not ordered it, and it would be nearly impossible to remove the gravel without damaging the existing driveway. Consequently, the company had to give the delivered gravel to the unintended address. They also had to make good on the original delivery request to the South Circle customer. This was embarrassing and costly.

The problem occurred because of a faulty street address. The agreements had been made by phone, and the mistake was easy to make. The dispatcher had not asked for a color or description of the house for the delivery. If she had, maybe the mistake would have been noticed before the stone was unloaded. In this particular case, everything worked out. The original customer received his stone delivery one day late, and the friend agreed to pay for the stone, even though he hadn't ordered it. The company gave him the gravel at a discount, and everybody ended up happy.

This story is based on actual events, and the friend who received the unintentional delivery was my father. This was my first exposure to the need for clear, concise, written agreements. I was only a child, but the memory stuck with me. I'm sure this experience has saved me thousands of dollars over the years. I learned first-hand about the importance of good property descriptions. This case involved less than a thousand dollars and the surface of a driveway. It could have involved much more. Imagine my father's reaction if he had found all his roof shingles removed or half of the house repainted! How can you keep a job on schedule when workers or materials are going to the wrong property? Don't underestimate the need for clear, legal property descriptions in your contract.

Scope of Work

The next element of the contract is the scope of the work. The information in this section will vary from trade to trade. This is where you describe the material to be supplied and the work to be done. Be specific. Some ideas of what to include are as follows:

- Model numbers
- Brands
- Lumber grades
- Colors

Leave nothing to the imagination when detailing specifications. This is the body of the contract. Name every item to be installed. Don't take anything for granted, and refer to a set of attached plans and specifications.

Elaborate on any areas or items that seem vague or confusing. Spend enough time on this section to be totally satisfied with your job description. If you aren't thorough here, the contractor can run rampant. This is where you can assure quality products and service. To keep your job running smoothly and on budget, you must ensure against misunderstandings and human error. Without the proper wording, your job can slide downhill fast.

It is not enough to say that you want the contractor to supply and install a white shower. You need to reference the location of the shower, as shown on your plans. The type and model number, as listed on your specifications, should also be detailed. You spent considerable time preparing your plans and specs, and in the contract your efforts will pay off.

In the scope of work section you can simply require all work to be done in compliance with the attached plans and specifications. If the plans and specs are done correctly, this is all you have to say. Mention in the contract that the attached plans and specs will be signed by all parties. Have the contractor review and sign the plans and specs before you release the contract. This removes any doubts about which plans and specs go with the contract. If you are dealing with several subcontractors, make sure each contract has a legible set of plans and specs attached. Many homeowners will reproduce their blueprints on a copying machine to save money on drafted duplicates. This only saves you money if the copies are complete and easy to understand. I have seen many copied plans that were too light to read or had vital information blurred or blanked out. Another drawback to photocopied plans is distortion; these copied plans cannot be used to make scale measurements.

Contract Changes

The next clause will deal with contract changes. This section should clearly state your position on deviations from the contract. Oral agreements should not be valid; require all changes to be in writing. Protect yourself from surprise billings with extravagant extras by stating your right to dishonor any claims unsubstantiated in writing. If you get such bills, you won't have to pay them unless a change order was issued and signed. This one clause can save you hundreds or even thousands of dollars. Don't omit it. It protects you from unauthorized additional expenses.

Written change orders protect the contractors, too. They know if they are asked to do additional work that it will be detailed in the change order. The terms of payment will also be specified. The contractors know they are assured of getting paid the correct amount when the terms are in writing. All too often, a customer will request additional work, then deny authorization for payment. These are usually small changes the customer assumed would be done as part of the original price. This problem won't exist when change orders are used.

Written change orders provide you with a simple way to control your budget and job progress. If a change must be made, find out how it will affect the other trades involved in the job. In this way, you eliminate the risk of agreeing to a change, only to discover tha it will throw the entire project off schedule. You can also negotiate alteration costs in advance, and weigh the effect on your budget in advance.

> Changes orders provide you with a checks and balances system, which will keep job costs from getting out of control.

Contractors will want exclusions in the contract and may attempt to include extensive latitude in a contract you provide. It is not unreasonable to allow some of these clauses. Contractors have to protect themselves from homeowners and guard against unknown conditions. You can count on resistance to your contract if you don't allow some exclusions. Contractors may even want you to waive them from liability for some aspect of a job. Try to get the contract signed without exclusions. If you can't, agree to include an addendum for the exclusions.

What are exclusions? Exclusions protect the contractor from certain circumstances. They deal with existing conditions and

CONTRACTOR EXCLUSION ADDENDUM

This exclusion addendum shall become an integral part of the contract, dated August 15, 2004, between the customer, Mr. & Mrs. J. P. Homeowner, and the contractor, Anytime Plumbing & Heating, for the work to be performed on Mr. & Mrs. J. P. Homeowner's residence. The residence and job location is located at 135 Hometown street, in the city of Wahoo, State of Vermont. The following exclusions are the only exclusions to be made. These exclusions shall become a part of the original contract and may not be altered again without written authorization from all parties.

THE EXCLUSIONS

Anytime Plumbing & Heating Company will provide for trenching the inside of the foundation for underground plumbing. If the trenching is complicated by rock, unusual depth, or other unknown factors, there will be cause for additional charges. The homeowner shall have the right to contract a different company to remove these obstacles, without affecting the agreed upon price between the homeowner and Anytime Plumbing & Heating Company. Anytime Plumbing & Heating Company will provide these services, if requested, in writing, at an hourly rate of $50.00 per hour.

Anytime Plumbing & Heating Company will provide roof flashings for all pipes penetrating the roof, but will not be responsible for their installation.

All trenching outside of the foundation will be provided by others.

The above exclusions are the only exclusions allowed to the contract between the two parties. There are no verbal agreements. This two-page document represents the whole agreement between the parties, as it pertains to exclusions.

ACCEPTANCE

We the undersigned do hereby agree to and accept all the terms and conditions of this addendum. We fully understand the terms and conditions and hereby consent to enter into this contract addendum.

Anytime Plumbing & Heating Company   Customer #1

by _____

Title _____   Date _____

by _____   Customer #2

                                            Date _____

Your Company Name
Your Company Address
Your Company Phone and Fax Numbers

LIABILITY WAIVER FORM

Customer: _____

Customer address: _____

Job name: _____

Job address: _____

I, _____, (Customer) hereby
acknowledge and accept the following: _____
_____
_____
_____
_____
_____
_____
_____
_____
_____
_____
_____
_____
_____
_____
_____

_____   _____
Customer   Contractor

_____   _____
Date   Date

unknown conditions. Carpenters want exclusions dealing with your existing structure. If a carpenter finds rotted structural members, he will want to be protected from having to replace them. The exclusions may address your existing second-floor joists or your unseen exterior wall structure. Since these are items that cannot be seen, they can't be planned for. You will have to be reasonable on these exclusions. You can't expect a carpenter to venture blindly into a termite-ridden house and make it structurally sound without additional charges.

> There have to be limits to exclusions. If the exclusion can be removed by a site inspection, don't allow the clause. As an example, an electrician might try to exclude responsibility for the adequacy of your existing electrical service. This is ridiculous. With a site inspection a competent electrician can evaluate your electrical service and determine if the service is adequate to support the proposed changes. Don't let contractors walk all over you with exclusions.

For a plumber, the exclusions will deal with your existing plumbing system. The plumber has no way of knowing if your sewer is filled with tree roots. He or she will not guarantee the installation to work properly if existing conditions prevent proper drainage. This is a legitimate exclusion. The same is true of water pressure. If your house has undersized water pipe, the plumber's new installation can't work to its full potential.

A carpenter who is too lazy to crawl under your house and examine existing conditions is not entitled to an exclusion. When an exclusion concerns the existing floor structure, it should only be allowed for areas without access to an inspection. A good carpenter can tell a lot about your home from visible signs. He or she can judge the depth of your exterior walls by probing around electrical outlets and measuring windows. This gives much of the information needed for structural planning. It is easy to estimate the size of

> You are contracting professional remodelers; make sure they have confidence in themselves. If they doubt their own ability, how can you have confidence in them?

floor joists with a few simple measurements, and a good remodeler can make very educated guesses. More often than not these guesses will be correct. The point is not to be too free to allow exclusions.

Payment Schedule

When you get to the price and payment schedule, take your best shot. Make the contract tight. Don't give in on any points unless you have to. Be prepared to compromise, but don't volunteer paying for services yet to be rendered. Start by offering payment upon completion. Make the contractor rebuttal this clause. The less you offer in the beginning, the more you have to bargain with later. Try to avoid giving deposits until after material is delivered and work is started. Strive to pay as little as possible with each phase. Appear confident that other contractors will accept your terms and play your hand to the end. If you really want particular contractors, give only what you have to in order to retain their services.

Start-and-Stop Date

Include a start-and-stop date as a time frame for the work to be completed. If you don't know exactly when the job will start, give the contractor a specified period of time to begin. For example, you could require the contractor to start the work within four days of your notification. On the day the contractor begins the job, ask him to sign a contract addendum listing the commencement date. The time frame you establish in the contract for his phase of the job will begin with this date.

Time is of the essence. These five simple words carry a lot of weight. They cement the importance of complying with a required time frame. Without the time-is-of- the-essence clause, your time requirements don't have as much weight. You must regulate the individual production components to keep your entire project on schedule. Even if you use a general contractor, be certain to include time parameters and a completion clause. An attorney can explain further the importance of such language in your contract.

If the ability to make money is a strong motivator, then the threat of losing money is even more powerful. Including a daily cash penalty clause for each day your completion agreement is not met will enforce your production requirements. Check with your attorney to see if this type of clause is acceptable in your jurisdiction. The amount of the penalties is up to you and the contractor to decide. For subcontractors, I use $100 per day. For a general contractor, I would suggest a minimum charge of $250 per day. This clause will almost guarantee an expedient job, but you must be fair in the time allowed for completion. This can be accomplished by asking the contractor how long the work will take. Adding one week to the time given by the contractor will establish a reasonable time for completion. Be prepared for resistance to this clause.

Even after contractors tell you how long the job will take, they will squirm when you include a penalty clause. Don't eliminate the clause. Extend it if you must, but don't remove it. A competent contractor will be willing to commit to a reasonable completion schedule. If the contractor refuses to allow any penalty clause, look for another contractor. This one obviously doesn't have faith in his abilities. Any good contractor will know approximately how long his job will take.

State in the contract that these penalty charges will be deducted from monies owed to the contractor. Without this stipulation, you will have to pay the contractor in full for the contract amount and then pursue the contractor for payment of the penalty. Good luck. Getting a contractor to pay you is tough. This is a losing proposition. Make arrangements to deduct penalties from the money owed; it's much easier to collect.

The only reasons for contractors to refuse a penalty clause are incompetence or bad intentions. This clause prevents your project from dragging on for months. If the job does run late, at least you are financially compensated for the inconvenience.

If the contractor protests that unforeseen problems will affect his completion projections, take the objection away. Explain to the contractor that your change order clause requires written agreement as to the time and costs to perform any additional work. This means that if he runs into legitimate problems, the completion date will be extended by the time frame specified in the change order. He is protected from the unknown, and your time-is-of-the-essence and penalty clauses protect you from costly delays. Creating an amicable contract for all parties concerned will keep your contractors honest and your job on schedule.

Your money is the best tool you have for controlling a contractor. Never let the contractors have the upper hand, and keep them leveraged into the job until the end. If the contractor has money invested, he will work to get it returned. If the remodeler is holding your money, he has little reason to work. This power is won or lost in the contract. Maintaining control is critical to your job, and money is critical to maintaining control. The contract will be your vehicle of control, but without the proper clauses you won't be able to maintain dominance. Spend enough time on the contract to avoid a regrettable job.

ON THE JOB

Once you have signed contracts in hand, you are ready to start the work. If you have a general contractor, all you have left to do is authorize the starting date. You can go about your daily life, and leave the details of the job to the general contractor. You don't have to do much, except inspect the work and write checks. Your penalty and production clauses will force the general contractor to expedite subcontractors and materials. He will be responsible for keeping the job on track. If subcontractors don't show up, the general will have to deal with the problems. When the wrong material is shipped, the general will take care of it. Your part in the job is minimal during the

INSPECTION LOG

Phase	Ordered	Approved

remodeling or construction process. Usually the less you do, the quicker and better the job will go.

You can be of the greatest assistance by making notes of any problems or questions you might have. Go over these notes with the general contractor. You may have discovered flaws he didn't know about. You are paying the general contractor to handle the job, so let him do it.

> Homeowners can get in the way and slow production down. If you are using a general contractor, let him earn his money. Leave the daily worries and work to the contractor, but look everything over at the end of the day. The workers will be gone and you won't be in the way.

There is no shame in hiring a professional. Remodeling is a tough business, and some of the people in the business are rough characters. It can be very intimidating to walk up to a 320-pound bricklayer and tell him his work isn't satisfactory. General contracting is not a job for everyone. You have to be firm and most of all you have to maintain control over the job. You can't allow vendors to get the better of you. At some point they are going to try to convince you to ignore the rules of remodeling. If you allow this to happen, you are going to lose the contest. Stick to the rules and stay on top of the job.

If you are going to act as your own general contractor, your responsibilities will be ongoing. After all your contracts are negotiated, you have to obtain your permits and order material. You must have the right material available when the subcontractors need it. Scheduling subcontractors will start out easy, but will certainly become complicated before the job is done. You will base your schedule on the intended completion dates given for each phase of the work. This will look good on the calendar, but you will inevitably have to change your schedule often. Some potential problems to be aware of include the following:

- A material delivery will be wrong or delayed.
- If you wait too long to place an order, work will have to stop.

- A subcontractor will run into unexpected problems with existing conditions and be slowed down. You will have to reschedule the other subs and material deliveries.

- The construction of additions and garages can be put on hold by inclement weather. Every day of production you lose is a day you have to call the subs.

- Damp, humid conditions can prevent your drywall mud from drying. The drywall process is time-consuming to start with. When complicated by the effects of damp weather, it can feel like an eternity. These are unavoidable delays.

It is your job as the general to maintain a smooth production schedule. I believe this is the hardest part of being a general contractor. The general has very little personal control over the events affecting a job schedule. All a good general can do is react quickly and effectively. With some foresight and effective planning, some of the delays can be avoided. Weather is uncontrollable, so all the general can do is develop a contingency plan. If weather will affect a trade, such as roofing, allow for weather in the contract. Adding a little heat in the room will help the drywall mud to dry. Tarps may make it possible for trades such as carpenters or siding subs to work in the rain.

Something will happen to disrupt even the best schedule.

You may have to cancel a material order. If you do, cancel it in writing to be sure that you will not be held responsible for the cost of materials that you don't need. If you run into materials that must be backordered, document the situation well. When you have to demand a delivery, document it. Rejecting orders is another fact of life. When you run into this situation, reject the goods in a formal manner. You may also encounter a time when you want to make a partial payment for materials. To stay out of trouble with your suppliers, provide written notice of which specific accounts you are paying on.

MATERIAL ORDER LOG

SUPPLIER: _____

DATE ORDER WAS PLACED: _____

TIME ORDER WAS PLACED: _____

NAME OF PERSON TAKING ORDER: _____

PROMISED DELIVERY DATE: _____

ORDER NUMBER: _____

QUOTED PRICE: _____

DATE OF FOLLOW-UP CALL: _____

MANAGER'S NAME: _____

TIME OF CALL TO MANAGER: _____

MANAGER CONFIRMED DELIVERY DATE: _____

MANAGER CONFIRMED PRICE: _____

NOTES AND COMMENTS

_____

_____

_____

_____

_____

_____

_____

At this point, you may be wondering why your contract should include so many protection clauses. Knowing there will be obstacles beyond your control, you must guard against situations you can control. Even with the best contract in the world, you have no guarantees that problems will not develop. What you do have is protection from unnecessary delays and contractor deceptions. Contracts will bridle unfair practices, and contingency plans will allow you to deal with the unexpected.

Your Company Name
Your Company Address
Your Company Phone and Fax Numbers

CANCEL ORDER

Date: _____

To: _____
     _____
     _____

I refer to our purchase order or contract dated _____, 20 _____, as attached.

Under said order, the goods were to be shipped by _____, 20 ___.

Because you failed to ship the goods within the required time, we cancel the order and reserve such further rights and remedies as we may have, including damage claims under the Uniform Commercial Code.
   If said goods are in transit, they shall be refused and returned at your expense under your shipping instructions.

Sincerely,

_____

Title: _____

Your Company Name
Your Company Address
Your Company Phone and Fax Numbers

CANCELLATION OF
BACKORDERED GOODS

Date: _____

To: _____
      _____
      _____

BE IT KNOWN, that pursuant to our purchase order dated
_____, 20 _____, as attached, we have received only a
partial shipment. As noted by you on the packing invoice, some
goods are out of stock or backordered.

   Please be advised that we are canceling the backordered goods.
Invoice us only for the goods received. If the backordered goods
are in transit, please advise us at once and we shall give you
further instructions.

Sincerely,

_____

Title: _____

Your Company Name
Your Company Address
Your Company Phone and Fax Numbers

DEMAND FOR DELIVERY

Date: _____

To (Supplier): _____

_____

_____

The Undersigned has paid you $_____ for goods to be shipped pursuant to our accepted order dated _____, 20_____; and we therefore demand delivery of said goods in accordance with our order.

Unless these goods are received by us on or before _____, 20 _____, we shall consider you in breach and demand full refund, reserving all other rights under the Uniform Commercial Code.

Please notify us of your intentions.

Sincerely,

_____

Title: _____

Your Company Name
Your Company Address
Your Company Phone and Fax Numbers

REJECTION OF GOODS

Date: _____

To: _____
_____

_____

We received goods from you under our order or contract dated _____, 20 _____. However, we reject said goods for the reason(s) checked below:

___ Goods failed to be delivered within the required contract time.

___ Goods were defective or damaged as described on attached sheet.

___ Goods did not conform to sample or specifications as described on attached sheet.

___ Confirmation accepting our order, as required, has not been received, and we therefore ordered the goods from another supplier.

___ Prices for said goods do not conform to quote, catalog, or purchase order price.

___ Partial shipment only received; we do not accept partial shipments.

___ Other (please see attached sheet).

Please provide instructions for return of said goods at your expense. Rejection of said goods shall not waive any other claim we may have.

Sincerely,

_____

Title: _____

Your Company Name
Your Company Address
Your Company Phone and Fax Numbers

PAYMENT ON SPECIFIC ACCOUNTS

Date: _____

To: _____

_____

_____

Our enclosed check number _____ for $_____
should be credited to the following charges or invoices only:

Invoice/Debt	Amount
	$

Payments herein shall be applied only to those specified items
listed and shall not be applied, in whole or in part, to other
obligations.

Sincerely,

_____

Title: _____

One of the by-products of polite negotiations is the large list of subcontractors and suppliers you develop. Having a wide selection of subcontractors available helps to reduce the effects of undependable workers. If a subcontractor leaves you high and dry in the middle of a job, you can approach the next best contractor on your list. You may have to accept a less than ideal agreement with the new sub, but you avoid having the job come to a standstill. Knowing where alternate materials can be purchased defuses some supplier-related problems.

Include a clause in your contract to allow you to use these alternate subs if the primary sub doesn't perform properly. Properly wording the clause can allow you to deduct any additional expenses you incur by using the replacement contractor from the original sub's bill. Follow the job closely and always look ahead. Your organizational skills will be your best weapon in the war against time.

If your project falls behind schedule, you will lose money. If contractors are able to hit you with extra charges, it will cost you money. A thorough contract, complemented by written agreements, will help protect against costly problems. Keeping your contractors honest isn't difficult. It is a simple matter of basic knowledge and written agreements. You can get all the knowledge you need from books, and written documentation will do the rest. You must exhibit strong confidence and conviction to your contractors. The way you present yourself will have a lot of bearing on who controls the job. Written agreements give you the basis for control, but it is up to you to exercise the control.

> Professional general contractors have the experience and contacts to overcome unexpected problems. Most homeowners don't have this advantage. Your best defense will be a good offense. Plan everything well in advance. Order your materials early and check each shipment for accuracy. Plan for problems and have backup subcontractors for each phase of the work.

9

Remodeling Rip-Offs

The title of this chapter says it all. It is a compilation of schemes to take your money. All the accounts represent circumstances that could happen to you. People think disasters only happen to the other guy. The purpose of this chapter is to illustrate how effectively professional con artists can take advantage of you. When you enter the realm of remodeling, you need to have your eyes and ears open. This is a field tainted by bad operators. Some of the people posing as remodeling contractors are blatant frauds. Your money and your house are at stake. Don't allow room for errors; there will be plenty of mistakes made without inviting them.

The people you want to deal with are professionals. Using the proper screening procedures, they will be quality remodelers. Without caution, they may be rip-off artists. Your knowledge and judgment will be tested to determine what kind of professional you are dealing with. After 30 years in the business, I have seen and heard the majority of the horror stories.

Here are some examples of these stories. I am going to relate them in a first-person style. Many are based on true events, and some are taken from personal experience. The true scenarios are mixed with hypothetical situations to protect the parties involved. The first one starts like this:

CASE HISTORY NUMBER ONE

I was hired to work for an established remodeling contractor to increase the company's volume of business. My position involved many tasks, but sales were my primary objective. When I was offered the position, the owner showed me the company's gross sales for the previous year. This business was a small one, owned and operated by an individual. The company had only grossed about $125,000 in the last year. The owner's goal was to reach a quarter of a million dollars in sales for the coming year.

The position fitted my personality. I could come and go as I pleased. The only requirement was producing sales. This was easy for me; I had been selling remodeling jobs for years. I designed a marketing plan for my new employer. It was based on direct mail, television, radio, telemarketing, and door-to-door campaigns. Our goal was to convey an image of success through extensive advertising.

Previously the company had relied on Yellow Page ads, an occasional ad in the newspaper, and word-of-mouth referrals. The owner worked on most of the jobs. They ran smoothly, and the quality of the work was good. I was impressed with the quality control and felt this could be a career with a bright future. Selling for a respected contractor would be easy. I had plenty of happy customers to give for references, and the company enjoyed a good business rating with no complaints. This was a salesperson's dream come true.

The public knew and respected this remodeler. He was well established and enjoyed an excellent reputation in the best neighborhoods. He worked from his home to keep his overhead low. The contractor enjoyed being on the job and talking with the homeowner. This is a real confidence builder. When homeowners can talk with the owner of the company, they feel secure. My job couldn't have been easier. My sales leads were provided to me, and I went out and sold the jobs.

The combination of the company's good reputation and my well-honed skills produced a high volume of sales. I was closing between 50 and 65 percent of all the estimate requests I went on. I was collecting large deposits with every job sold, and this cash injection fueled the growth of the company. The owner added new employees, new trucks, and rented a commercial space for the office and warehouse. He hired a full-time secretary and increased my advertising budget.

The additional advertising brought in more estimate requests. I arranged for the company to be an authorized dealer of on-the-spot financing. With the addition of easy financing, the sales figures ballooned. The company had more work than it could do, and cash was flooding in. Based on the sales after only six months, the company would gross over $500,000 by the end of the year.

The owner had only aimed for $250,000; now it looked like we could easily double that figure. I was a hero; my efforts had catapulted the business into the major leagues. At this point you are probably wondering how this success relates to fraudulent contractors. You are about to see an example of the importance of looking below the surface of a company.

From outside appearances this contractor was reaching the pinnacle of quality contractors. He had been in business for years and was growing. There were many jobs in progress, and the company showed signs of thriving. This successful appearance made customers comfortable and confident in the company. Unfortunately, there were several changes happening within company, but the public only saw the surface.

> Don't always believe what you see. A company or contactor who appears successful on the outside could be deeply in debt. This may result in difficulty getting your job completed.

Rapid growth had forced the owner to hire new employees, and there wasn't time to screen them. To meet production schedules, the company needed workers on the jobs immediately. These workers were not capable of producing the quality of work the company was known for. The inexperience of the new help showed in the work, and jobs in progress were starting to suffer. The owner had his hands full, scheduling work and paying bills. The lack of his presence at the jobs encouraged lower quality in the work. Homeowners were frustrated, because they could no longer talk with the owner. He didn't return their phone calls and only went to the job to collect money.

All the new company acquisitions were financed or paid for from the general operating account. The overhead of the company rose rapidly, and the company's growing pains were transferred to the customers. The expansion was gaining momentum, and the owner no longer had a clear concept of the requirements of each job. On the surface, potential customers were still impressed with the company, and sales were still on the rise.

Then two changes took place, which would be the beginning of the end for the contractor. First, the owner started to believe that he was going to be rich. The company bank account was larger than ever before. He could not recognize that this was the result of large deposits, collected for jobs that had not yet started. With this newfound artificial wealth, the owner stumbled. He became involved with drugs and worsened the situation. He lost his perspective on the customers and their jobs. His only focus was on the customer's money. I could see that the company was in deep trouble and spent hours trying to reason with the owner. My suggestions were ignored, and the problems continued to build.

> Avoid giving large deposits to contractors before materials are delivered and work is done. Some contractors will keep the deposit without fulfilling contract commitments.

Roofs were leaking, jobs were not being finished, and customer complaints were growing. The owner spent most of his time trying to find ways to avoid customers and bill collectors. The contractor began to insist on excessive deposits for every job. Deposits were being spent on everything except the people's jobs. The company's credit had been cancelled with many suppliers, due to late payments. When the time came to buy material for a job, there was no money. The owner got caught up in the thrill of success but was unwilling to take the necessary steps to ensure continued success. When the owner insisted that I sell more jobs than our schedule could accommodate, I resigned.

The customers were hurt in many ways. Some jobs were never finished. Many jobs never started even after deposits were taken. The quality of the work was below industry standards, and eventually there was no company left to maintain warranty work. This was a disaster; everyone lost. There was very little warning to the customers, and the business went down fast. How can you protect yourself from the whirlwind destruction of a seemingly reputable contractor? Here are a few suggestions for staying safe when dealing with contractors:

- First, do your homework.
- Require current references.
- Check references personally.
- Get everything in writing.
- Avoid large deposits.
- Don't advance money until work is completed to your satisfaction.
- Inspect all work closely.
- Require lien waivers to be signed with every cash disbursement.
- Never assume anything.

CASE HISTORY NUMBER TWO

This story was told to me by a homeowner. The homeowner called me for an estimate on a new sunroom. The homeowner really grilled me, asking more questions and requesting more verifications than you can imagine. I thought that it was unusual that she knew to ask such pertinent questions and asked her why she was requiring this amount of detail. Her answer was simple. She had just been defrauded by a so-called contractor and had learned from experience. This experience was costly but left an impression she wouldn't soon forget.

In her case, the woman called a contractor from a classified ad in the newspaper. She wanted to save money and thought the contractors in the paper would be less expensive. The contractor came out and gave her a quote on the work. He then said that he could do the job for less if she supplied the material. The contractor explained that his cost would be less if he didn't have to supply the material. He gave several reasons to justify the price reduction, and the homeowner thought she had made a good deal.

> Whenever possible, be on your jobsite. Being present during deliveries and work can reduce your risk considerably.

> Contractors who advertise in newspapers and who are not in local phone directories may not be established. This does not mean that they are not good contractors, but it is a red flag that you should investigate.

The contractor took out a form contract and filled in the appropriate information. It was a very simple one-page proposal, which covered all the normal items. After all, the homeowner was supplying the material, and the proposal was for labor only. The customer signed the proposal and gave the contractor a $2,000 deposit. They agreed that the work would start on the following Monday to allow time for the homeowner to have the material delivered.

Monday morning found the material and the contractor on the job. It looked like everything was going according to plan. The contractor had a cup of coffee and discussed the job with the customer. Then the customer had to go to work, and the contractor walked out with her to inspect the material. All the material was stacked in the front yard. There were high-quality sliding glass doors, expensive casement windows, and framing lumber. The homeowner drove away, and the contractor got busy sorting material.

When the customer returned home, she was pleasantly surprised to see how much of the material had been used. Since the room was being built in the rear of the house, the material had to be moved to the location. Excited to see how much work was done, she dashed around the house. Turning the corner, she was shocked with disbelief. The job hadn't been started, but the material was gone. It took some time for the reality of the situation to sink in; she was a victim of fraud.

The so-called contractor had taken a $2,000 deposit when she signed the proposal and had maneuvered her into supplying over $6,000 worth of material. Now she was out $8,000 and had no idea how to find the rip-off artist. The phone number she called was an answering service, and the address on the proposal turned out to be bogus. She didn't even have a clear recollection of the truck he was driving. It could have been rented under a false name. This type of dilemma isn't common, but it can happen. What did she do wrong? Here are some examples of her mistakes:

- She made a snap decision to sign the proposal.
- The deposit was too large a sum, especially for a labor-only contract.
- References were neither requested nor checked.
- Placing all the material on the job at one time increased her risk.
- She didn't verify the contractor's state or local license.

Not all remodeling rip-offs are on such a grandiose scale. Most remodeling fraud is done in much smaller quantities. It is harder to detect, and the guilty contractor can continue to operate in the same location, despite adverse business practices. If the contractor's actions are exposed, restitution is usually made without a lot of publicity. Some contractors may not even consider their actions as wrong. There are other types of activities that also affect the consumer. While not direct fraud, they are deviations from verbal commitments. Such unprofessional acts continue to hurt the image of remodeling contractors. A classic example is known as job juggling.

JOB JUGGLING

Job juggling is a frequent complaint of homeowners involved with contractors. It may be hard to believe, but general contractors are also constant victims of job juggling from subcontractors. When a general contractor is subjected to job juggling from a sub, the homeowner feels the effect. A general contractor is only as good as the subcontractors working under his or her supervision. The promises made to you by a general are based on commitments made to him from the subcontractors.

> The quickest way for a remodeler to generate cash is by job juggling. The consumer suffers, their job is prolonged, completion dates aren't met, and inconveniences arise.

Job juggling is difficult to avoid. Contractors want to stay busy, and to do so they take several jobs within the same time frame. When these jobs get out of sync or cash flow problems occur, job juggling results. When bills come due, a contractor has to generate cash. This is especially true of companies without a cash reserve to operate with.

Job juggling is the art of moving from job to job, doing as little as necessary, to generate cash. This can mean contracting new jobs to obtain deposit money or doing just enough work on a project to receive a draw. Sometimes job juggling is used as a facade to make the customer happy. They see workers on the job, these workers are only there to make an appearance. They may leave after an hour or two, but the contractor can honestly say he had workers on the job.

Some contracts require the contractor to work on the job every day, and job juggling meets this requirement. The workers may not get much work done, but they are there every day. The intent behind this clause is to expedite the job, but it falls short due to creative job juggling. This problem can be solved with clauses requiring a definite date of completion and penalties for delays. Job juggling loses its effectiveness in the face of clauses such as these.

The most common reason for job juggling is cash flow. Contractors send in crews to do just enough to be eligible for a cash advance. For example, if your contract authorizes a payment when drywall is hung, that's all the contractor has to do. The drywall doesn't have to be taped, and they don't have to apply the first coat of joint compound. All they have to do is hang it and collect their cash. You have to pay for this minimal effort, because the contract says you will.

Logic dictates that doing as much as possible in every trip to a job is the most cost-effective approach. After all, money is lost in travel time and loading and unloading tools. Why would a contractor only hang the drywall and leave when he could tape and coat it, in the same day? The need to generate cash often overpowers logic. The contractor can spend half the day on your job and half a day on another job and get two checks instead of one.

This type of scheduling is expensive for the contractor and inconvenient for the customer. The contractor knows that he is losing money by working in this manner. He also knows the customer will not stay happy for long when subjected to these work habits. Even with this knowledge, contractors still perform the "Now you see them, now you don't" game. You can eliminate job juggling with a strong completion clause in your contract.

The clause will include a start and completion date. It will allow you to charge the contractor a penalty fee for every day the completion date is exceeded if this practice is legal and recommended in your jurisdiction. The clause should allow you to deduct these penalty fees from the money you owe the contractor. You should also include the option of bringing in another contractor to complete the work if the production schedule is not adhered to. With proper wording you can deduct the new subcontractor's charges from money owed to the original sub. The threat of losing the job to someone else and of having to pay that person to take his work will effectively deter a contractor from job juggling.

Seek legal advice on the proper clauses to include in your contracts to prevent job juggling.

LOW BIDS

Another unfair business practice involves the manipulation of a homeowner by offering a known low bid. This is performed by contractors who will give you a very good price just to get your job. They appear to be the best value of all the contractors bidding the work. You award the job to the low-bid contractor and commend yourself for the money you are saving. This can be a short-lived, false sense of satisfaction.

This group of cutthroat contractors is expert at going in as the low bidder and walking away with the most profit. How can that be possible? By substituting material and charging extra for work you assumed was included in the original price. They can maneuver you into a position of either accepting their terms or spending several months in litigation to resolve the conflict.

In the beginning everything will appear normal. The contractor will give you the contract to sign and tell you how happy you will be with the job. He will usually emphasize the amount of money you will be saving by using him. He is a real contractor and appears as reputable as any of the others you have interviewed. When you sign the contract, you lose control. He is now telling you what you will get. The terms will be ambiguous, and many of the promises will only be verbal.

You review the contract and question the inclusion of a clause about substituting materials. If your plans and specification are incorporated into the contract, why does the agreement include a substitution clause? The contractor may try to characterize this clause as a safeguard to protect against job delays. He will verbally explain that substitutions will only be made if the original items aren't readily available when needed.

Of course, the clause doesn't specify what the replacements will be. It only says the material may be substituted with a similar product. While a toilet is a toilet, the quality, size, and price can differ dramatically. A basic builder-grade toilet can be purchased for less than $70. The one you specified may sell for as much as $300. They are both toilets—both have a tank, a seat, and a bowl—but that is where the similarities end. If the contractor installed the builder-grade toilet, would you consider this substitution fair? Of course you wouldn't. You would demand the toilet you specified. The contractor would then remind you of the substitution clause and refuse to change the toilet. To settle this dispute, you would have to go to court. In the meantime, the contractor would lien your house for lack of payment. This gets expensive fast. The contractor knows your easiest alternative will be to accept the toilet. He has held you hostage with threats of a costly court battle and time delays. Now it becomes clear why the other contractor's prices

> If you encounter a contractor who insists on a substitution clause for materials in your contract, you have to make a decision. Will you accept this clause? Try not to. The clause can hurt you during the course of the job.

were higher. The contractor with the low bid never intended to use the more expensive toilet. When are substitution clauses acceptable?

- Substitution clauses are normal and often necessary.
- Determine how the clause deals with substitutions.
- Detail what the acceptable alternate choices will be if the original product is not available.
- Include make, model number, color, and any other descriptive language you can.
- Insist on a written change order authorizing necessary substitutions.
- Leave nothing open for interpretation or negotiation.
- Only allow substitution if a product is unavailable from at least three major suppliers.
- This type of wording will protect you from this bait-and-switch scam.

EXTRAS

Another game low-ball contractors play is adding up the extras. Once they have the job, they will start to take advantage of you. When you signed the contract, you questioned the light fixture allowance of $500. It didn't seem like enough. You were assured it would be sufficient, because you would be saving money by buying from the contractor's supplier. This made the contractor seem like a nice guy, saving you money by letting you get the fixtures at his builder cost. The contractor also said you could upgrade the fixtures later if you wanted to. You entered into the contract and planned your budget based on the contract amount.

When you went to select your light fixtures, you were appalled by the prices. Your $500 allowance would easily be depleted with the purchase of one chandelier. After an exhaustive inspection of the supplier's selection, you realized you would have to spend more than the allotted amount. You picked out what you wanted and the price was $875. Sure, the contractor allowed you to upgrade, but it cost you an extra $375. Now here is the real clincher. You thought getting the fixtures from the contractor's supplier meant you would get them at his cost. Wrong—he never said you would benefit from a price reduction, only that you could get the fixtures from his supplier. With the mark-up built into the light fixtures, the contractor picked up a nice profit from the extra cost.

This move wasn't illegal, and it didn't leave you much of a choice. You were in a bind. You needed the lights, but didn't want to cheapen your new space with plastic light fixtures. These contractors know how to play the game. This one tactic kept the original bid price $375 lower than the contractor's competitors. The agreement was in writing; what could you have done differently? You could have specified the light fixtures in advance. This would have removed the need for an allowance. Then you would have had what you wanted. The cost would have still been $875, but you would have known the cost before starting the job.

There are many other areas where extras can be added up. When you contracted the job, you expected doorknobs to be included with the doors. You didn't specify them in the contract because you assumed handles must come with the doors. The contract stipulated that the contractor would supply and install three hollow-core interior doors and two bifold closet doors. It didn't say anything about doorknobs or hardware. When this question comes up, what will the contractor say?

> Use strong, strict specifications when you put your job out to bid. Insist on having contractors bid jobs based on the specifications.

He will point out that you didn't specify these items and that you never questioned the contract. The contractor will try to convince you that he thought you were supplying the items. He may even complain that you are now trying to take advantage of him. This isn't a big expense, so you pay extra for the items. When this continues with other items, the extras add up. You can spend hundreds of dollars on small extras.

These unexpected costs will blow your budget out of the water. Now it is easier to see how the original bid was so low. These extras can be avoided with detailed specifications. The specifications should be made an integral part of your contract.

Being aware of potential risks is half the battle of avoiding them. Remodeling isn't destined to be a bad experience; the key is educating yourself and following the rules. There are some fraudulent contractors, but they are far outnumbered by reputable ones. Your odds of getting involved with a bad contractor will be minimized if you use the information you learn from this book.

Remodeling can be a fabulous experience. With the right contractors, you can enjoy seeing your dreams come to life. It's hard not to get excited about revamping your house. You can make all the changes you want and can afford. You won't have to put up with outdated features any longer. Coming home from work every day will be an adventure. You get to see how much of the remodeling work was done. All this excitement can cloud your judgment. Getting excited is part of the joy of remodeling, but it is important to keep your excitement under control. Corrupt contractors will play on your emotions and use them to take your money any way they can. Don't get sloppy in the middle of the job. Use the principles and knowledge you have taken the time to learn.

> Require written change orders for any deviation from the contract, including substitutions. These safeguards will keep your job on budget and lower your risks.

10

Making the Commitment

B y now you know more about remodeling than some contractors. You have learned all the basic elements required to plan a successful job. The expenses of remodeling have been discussed, and you know how to get the most for your money. The only hurdle standing between you and your remodeling dreams is the final decision. Now you must resolve to do the project and decide how to get the job done. For some, this will still be difficult. Your project may require a sizable investment. You have read the horror stories, and are not convinced the benefits outweigh the risks. In cases such as this, I recommend that you list the pros and cons of your project. Categorizing the information in black and white may surprise you. Reviewing the advantages and subsequent financial gains of your remodeling plans should you sell your home may eradicate your fears.

The best place to start is the beginning. Reconsider your qualifications to be your own general contractor. Now that you know what is required to run the job, do you feel competent to manage the entire project? Take the time to consider this decision thoroughly. Try to determine how qualified you are to run your own job. Organizational ability is the first quality to analyze. Are you confident that you can coordinate the whole job? How does your regular job compare with the skills needed to be a general contractor? Is your profession centered on personnel management?

This can be a big advantage when you tackle your remodeling project. If your daily job includes managing people, you have at least one of the needed qualities of a good general contractor. Managing and manipulating subcontractors will be similar to overseeing your employees. Subcontractors may present a bigger challenge, because they can be very independent and a little rough around the edges. Most of them can't be compared to the people you might manage in a dress shop or bank. Examine your overall aptitude to regulate and supervise other people's activities. Here are some questions to ask yourself when making this decision:

- Do you deal well with problems that catch you unprepared?

- Does your job require you to be a problem solver?

- Can you perform well under pressure?

- Do you tend to stress out easily, lose your temper, or become confused under pressure?

- In your job are you required to work with or assimilate intricate information?

- Do you take notes during your business phone calls?

- If you request information from another department at work, do you write down the name of the person you requested it from?

- At home do you keep your deposit slips to reconcile with your bank statement?

- For your receipts, which do you use: an organized filing system, the shoebox method, or the trashcan approach? If executing methodical plans and maintaining detailed documents doesn't suit your nature, hire a professional to manage your job.

- Are you the kind of person who carefully shops for the best prices?

- Will you dicker over prices at a craft fair, or do you simply not buy items that exceed your price range?

- During your last job interview, did you negotiate for the salary and benefits you wanted or accept what the boss offered?

* Do you emphasize your exemplary performance during a pay review or just welcome any raise you get?

- In general, how much do you know about remodeling and construction?

The average occupation will not provide you with the knowledge needed for the technical aspects of remodeling. But your business and personal traits will tell you a lot about your ability to act as your own general contractor. You don't have to be able to lay a brick foundation or solder pipes to manage a remodeling project. You only have to learn enough to keep the contractors in line. If you are willing to commit time to studying, you can pass the remodeling knowledge test.

> The ability to organize and manage people and events is one of the most important elements of a good general contractor.

FINANCING

Financing is one of the easier decisions to make. Be cautious about the documents you sign and do what suits you best. There is no big mystery to financing. If you need it, attempt to get it. If you don't need it, you have a choice. You can pay cash or finance the job to conserve your cash. Your lender will handle the details of arranging for financing. You only need to know how much you can afford and how long you are willing to make loan payments. After that you will simply compile and compare information from the many financing sources available. Once you find the program that best suits your needs, the lenders will handle the rest of the financing details for you.

The average homeowner can handle the financial aspects of contracting. There is no need for highly specialized knowledge here. You will need to determine preliminary cost parameters, which will be refined as you receive quotes on the project. Accurate expense projections must include both hard and soft costs. Amounts for everything from permits to carpet must be incorporated into your calculations. After you establish your finished budget, it will be crucial to stick to it. How are you at handling money? Will you be able to account for expenses and keep track of costs throughout your job's progression?

> Regardless of whether you use a general contractor or coordinate the work yourself, you must be able to keep your job on budget.

TIME

Will you have enough time to run the job? Plan on a few hours each day. Some days will require more time than others, depending on the size of the job, the trades involved, and your organizational skills. If you can handle the responsibilities of general contractor, you will enjoy a handsome savings on the cost of your job. If you have any doubts at this point, call in a professional to manage the job. The extra cost will be worth it to enjoy a job well done.

SCOPE OF WORK

What is the scope of the work to be done? Take this opportunity to review your design ideas. Are you sure you're happy with your designs? Once you are into the job, making changes will be costly and inconvenient. If it's been awhile since you looked at the design, you may take one look and have several new ideas. Since your original design you have investigated a lot of new products. Maybe you will want to incorporate these products into your design.

Double-check the design for accuracy. Don't build yourself into a money pit. Make the best use of your time and money by making any needed changes now. Don't wait until the final prints are drawn or the job is started. Your design decision is one you will live with for a long time. It will affect the resale value of your home.

Approaching remodeling with a casual attitude will result in disappointment. Altering your home is serious business, and major money can be made or lost. If it's done right, you will enjoy a healthy equity gain for your efforts. When you sell, this translates into profit.

> Don't make a hasty decision on the design. Study it carefully and be sure it is what you want. If the design doesn't excite you, it probably needs a few changes. Don't be blinded by excitement to the extent of investing in an undesirable improvement.

FINANCIAL GAINS

The financial gains of a well-designed improvement will figure prominently in your final decision. It can be like matching your investments with free money. You invest $10,000 and get an equity gain of $12,500. This means that you make $2,500 for improving your home, and you don't pay taxes on the profits until you sell the

> Remodeling is an excellent way to increase your family's nest egg. Can you think of a better way to make money than by improving your living conditions? With the right improvements the profits will stagger your imagination. You can have new space to enjoy and increase the value of your largest investment. If you act as your own general contractor, the profits go off the charts. Remodeling is one of the safest investments you can make, and most projects add value to your home.

house. Even then a good accountant can show you how to defer your tax consequences. Remodeling offers profits beyond your wildest dreams. When you add value to your home today, it should increase in all the future years of your homeownership.

Perhaps an example will make your decision easier to make. Assume you are considering an addition with a market value of $25,000, and you are the general contractor. Your immediate equity gain from being the general can amount to 20 percent of the value, or $5,000. To calculate your total profit ten years from now, you need to estimate the percentage amount by which property values, in your area will increase. We will assume the annual appreciation rate for your location is 7 percent. Annual appreciation varies greatly from location to location, but we will use 7 percent in our example. To determine your long-term gains, start to multiply each year's value by 7 percent. Be aware that this may not be an accurate number, but it will show you how to do the math when you use numbers that apply to your situation.

At the end of ten years, your $25,000 addition is worth over $49,000. Your instant equity was worth $5,000, and now you can add over $24,000 to that figure. Your total profit from the job is in excess of $29,000. This is a lot of money to earn for only a few months of part-time work. Moreover, all the time your investment was growing you were enjoying the benefits of the new addition. This is an unbeatable deal.

All you have to do is make the best use of your abilities. It's no different from jockeying for a promotion at work. The people who make their move and are qualified receive the financial rewards. If you choose the right remodeling project, you can hit the jackpot. Bringing the job to a successful conclusion will result in plentiful profit for a part-time effort.

The key to remodeling riches is choosing improvements that cost the least and add the most value.

ADDITIONS

New additions are especially suited for the part-time general contractor. They don't cause as much disruption to the basic operation of your household. You have the latitude to schedule and coordinate the job as time allows. Bathrooms and kitchens require an expeditious completion. You can't afford to have these areas out of service for an extended time. Additions are different. An addition can take sixty days or six months to complete. It won't have a negative effect on your home life during the construction. These projects offer the highest profits to the part-time contractor. You can save even more money by doing some of the construction and completion work yourself.

PLANS

For most projects the free plans offered by your material supplier will suffice. Talk with your potential supplier and verify his or her ability to provide your plans and specs. Confirm that the plans are in fact free-of-charge. It is usually

When you are satisfied with the feasibility of the project, concentrate on how to get it done. You will need finalized plans and specs. Do you want to pay an architect to develop them for you? The final decision on the use of an architect is a big one. If you can get what you want without using an architect, you will save significant money.

at the commitment stage that you will uncover any hidden charges for this service. Nobody gives you something for nothing. The price for the plans and specifications may be hidden in your material costs. Evaluate all the costs and be sure the plans are worth the overall expense. If the plans are truly available for free, give them a lot of consideration. The money saved here will go a long way with your project.

The chances are good that you can use the blueprints from a material supplier. They won't have as many details as architectural plans, but for simple projects they will get the job done. I don't like the specifications that accompany these free plans. They don't go into enough detail. Free plans and specs can't be beat for price, and many contractors use these same plans and specifications. There is nothing wrong with what you get. The problem lies in what you don't get. You cannot rely on the specifications provided with free plans.

Plan on writing your own specifications if you don't engage an architect. In most cases you will be able to prepare your own specs. Large projects involving engineered changes can require professional specifications. Before deciding against an architect, weigh the advantages to your individual situation.

Vague plans and specifications can ruin your project. They can cause your cost estimates to be well below actual cost. Don't save on your plans at the expense of your entire job.

Drafting companies are another alternative. These companies can provide you with quality prints to work from. They will include as much detail as you request. You will be charged for their services, but the expense should be much less than an architect. You will still be faced with the lack of custom specifications. The bottom line is: are you going to have time to create your specifications? Even with architects you will have to tell them what to include.

Evaluate your job and what you are willing to pay for the design phase of the project. If the job is really basic, you may be able to use your own line drawings. If the project is moderately simple, go with free plans. For jobs requiring extensive structural work, get good blueprints from either an architect or drafting firm. If your time is very valuable, architects may be the best solution. Be prepared to wait for professionally prepared plans.

Architects can have heavy backlogs of work, and getting architectural plans can take months. Drafting companies will probably produce your plans in just a few weeks. Lumberyards may be able to complete plans in a week or less. These time factors will have some influence on your decision. Explore all the facets of this important aspect, and do what you feel best about.

If you decide to use your preliminary line drawings, be sure to have the contractor review and approve them in writing. An experienced remodeler will know what work and code requirements are needed for most projects. Talk with your contractors and the code enforcement office. See if you really need elaborate blueprints for your project. If your job can be done from your own drawings, you will save even more time and money. If you decide to work from your line drawing, be sure it's accurate. Poorly drawn plans produce disappointments later.

PICKING CONTRACTORS

Picking contractors is the next step toward seeing your dream become a reality. At this point you are able to make the final decision on precisely what work to do and how to pay for it. The only step left is to determine exactly who to use in performing the work. Prices will tell you a lot, but don't be blinded by low bids. Make sure the low bids aren't too low. The contractor with extremely low bids isn't always the best value. Remember the story about the woman who lost her sunroom deposit and materials to the cheapest guy in town. The bid process isn't too complicated, but it is time-consuming.

You will have to meet with several people, and much of your time will be spent on the phone. Some of these calls will have to be done during normal working hours. Do you have the flexibility to make personal calls from work? If you don't have the time, hire a professional to handle the day-to-day complexities of remodeling.

Whether you are seeking a general contractor or a subcontractor, the principles are the same. Choosing your contractors is one of the hardest decisions you will have to make. You have to look at more than just prices. You need to match the right contractors to the right jobs.

Don't hire a framing specialist to install your intricate trim. Don't engage a commercial plumber for your residential remodeling job. You want to find contractors with extensive experience in the kind of work you want done. In heavily populated areas there will be specialists. In some cities plumbers specialize in bath and kitchen remodeling. They don't do repair work, install new construction, or handle commercial jobs. They work with bath and kitchen remodeling every day, and that is all they do. If you want to remodel your home's plumbing, these are the experts you want.

These specialized plumbers know their business. By doing the same thing every day, they have extensive experience in all phases of their work. Their counterparts do different types of plumbing. While a new construction plumber may know the basics of kitchen and bath remodeling, he or he isn't expert at it. When something goes wrong, he may not know how to correct the problem. The lack of experience in remodeling will cause difficulties the experts wouldn't have. A general plumber may overcompensate for his lack of remodeling experience in the price he gives you. In this case, the price will be much too high. If the job is underestimated, the plumber will have to cut corners to avoid losing money. You are always better off to engage experts whenever possible.

In rural areas, there isn't enough work to allow heavy specialization. Tradesmen must be able to do a wide variety of work. Your carpenter may have built a tool shed last week, flowerboxes the week before, and a garage just last month. Rural plumbing can include everything from stopped-up drains to installing hog-watering devices. When a contractor tells you that he has built garages before, ask him how many, when, and where? If the answer is one last year, for his uncle, you may need to get additional bids.

I once overheard a new construction carpenter complaining about interior remodeling. He didn't appreciate having to take off his work boots to go into a customer's home. When I rejected his bid to finish an attic, he couldn't understand why. I told him that I only use professionals who understand the importance of a clean job as well as clean carpets. The moral of the story is to use experienced professionals who prefer the kind of work you

All contractors will have personal preferences as to the type of work they like. Ask what kind of work they enjoy before you begin to describe the work you need. Make the closet match you can. By asking what they do best before describing your job, you will get more honest answers.

have to offer. You will get a better price and better quality from these contractors.

Think long and hard before committing to contractors. Be sure all your paper-work is in order. Don't make the contractor decision until you are convinced you have found the right people. Interview as many contractors as you can, and avoid making on-the-spot commitments. Check out the contractors and their work carefully. You can never be sure of your decision until the job is done. The best you can do is to avoid the common problems and be prepared to deal with the unknown ones.

The purpose of this chapter is to help you prepare for your final decisions. Up to this point, all the work has been administrative. Now the actual remodeling work can start. You are about to enter the working world of remodeling. This is where your extensive preparation and planning will pay off. Finally you will be able to see the design and specifications that you worked so hard on become a reality. The paper profit figures you generated, based on careful negotiations and thrifty shopping, are about to become concrete equity gains. Enjoy having made wise, profitable remodeling decisions. Chances are that you will have to make some on-the-spot decisions before the job is over. Until the unexpected happens, you can sit back and watch your project take shape.

11

On-the-Spot Decisions

Remodeling involves working with unknown conditions. When you open up a wall, you never know what you will find. I have discovered old money, wild animals, snakes, termite damage, and a host of other surprises. Existing conditions can wreak havoc with the best-laid remodeling plans. These unexpected complications dictate a change of strategy. Some of these problems will require fast decisions, either to save time or rectify an emergency. Remodeling crews are expensive; you can't afford for them to stand around very long. In most cases, you can protect against problems before they occur with a strong contract. If the unimaginable happens, the ability to reason through situations will enable you to make rational decisions.

The homeowner will be responsible for most on-the-spot decisions. It will be up to you to decide what should be done about the bats living in your attic. When the carpenters tell you about a problem, they expect an immediate resolution. When the subfloor in a bathroom is removed, many problems may be found. What will you do with rotted floor joists?

If your old toilet leaked, the water may have caused structural damage. The same problem can result from bad grouting around ceramic tile. The water can run down the walls and ruin the wall and floor structures.

Your initial plans to replace the vinyl floor and plumbing fixtures can turn into a full blown remodeling job. What started as a $2,000 job is now going to cost $6,000. This figure can go much higher if the bathroom is on the second floor. In this case, additional repairs would have to be done. If not, the damaged structure would give away at some point. Your bathtub could wind up under the house, or the toilet could drop through the ceiling into the kitchen. The repairs must be made, and you have to decide what to do. What would you do?

Beware of unseen problems associated with walls and floors.

This example is not unusual. Bathrooms hold a lot of moisture, and structural damage can go unnoticed for years. Something as simple as replacing a toilet can turn into a nightmare. When the toilet is removed, the plumber may discover rotted floor joists. Typically, it is only the subfloor that has been heavily damaged. If this is the case, consider yourself lucky. The cost to replace the subfloor and your vinyl floor covering will be around $1,500 or more. You were expecting a bill for $185 to replace your toilet. This scenario happens time and time again. Should you accept the facts and authorize the repairs? You know they have to be done, and the plumber is pressuring you for an answer. Wait—don't authorize anything yet.

What are the details of the work? The contractor says you will have to replace your entire subfloor, underlayment, and vinyl floor covering. He also points out the expense of removing the debris from your property. To do the job right, the plumber indicates he will have to remove your vanity until the new floor is installed. Then he will have to come back to reset the toilet and vanity. The carpenter tells you about the need to replace your baseboard trim. When the trim is replaced, it will need to be painted. The workers estimate the combined total cost but won't guarantee the price. You are told there could be more damage, so they can't commit to a quoted price. This is a bad decision.

At this point thank the contractors, and tell them you will get back to them with your decision. Get them out of the house, get away from the pressure, and think about the predicament. The urgency of the situation may make you feel that you have no choice but to have the contractor make the necessary repairs. Slow down, and go back over the techniques and rules you learned in putting your job out to bid. Would you accept the first bid without making any comparisons? No, the first order of business is to get other quotes. Call other contractors and ask what they will charge to make these repairs to your bathroom. Don't tell them what the first contractors said needed to be fixed. Let the new contractors tell you what work is required. I'm willing to bet that you will get several different answers.

Some remodelers will see this call as an opportunity to try to sell you on remodeling the whole bathroom. They will look at the subfloor and vinyl and tell you this is the perfect time to remodel. Since you are faced with extensive disruptive repairs, why not go ahead and do a complete remodel job? If you are planning to update the room in the future, this option may be worth considering. If remodeling the room is what you wand to do, fine, but don't be talked into doing more than you want or need to do. If you don't want to do a complete remodel job, ask the contractor to simply quote the work you called for.

One of the contractors should offer you the right

You may find a few contractors who suggests doing as little as possible. They will advise putting shims under a toilet to keep it from rocking. These face-lift contractors will give you ideas such as caulking around the base of the toilet and tub to reduce the moisture after structural damage has been done. The list of band-aid repairs will go on and on. Avoid these contractors—you will be paying them now only to pay a good contractor again in the future.

option. When you find an experienced contractor, he will be able to give you a viable choice. When toilets leak, the sub-floor starts to rot around the toilet. The water is absorbed into the floor and spreads. If this condition continues, eventually the floor joists will be damaged. The majority of toilet problems are noticed before severe structural damage occurs. Typical flooring repairs are simple.

The contractor should be able to cut out the bad section of subfloor and replace it with plywood. The repair doesn't have to involve removing your entire floor. The vinyl flooring will need to be replaced, but all the other major expenses can be avoided. You won't need new baseboard trim or painting. The vanity will not need to be removed. There won't be extensive debris to haul away. The amount of labor involved is greatly reduced, and the total cost of the repairs should be much less than some contractors will suggest.

Proper planning eliminates most on-the-spot decisions. Many of the problems that catch you off guard are a result of not thinking. Think your project through completely before starting the work.

PROBLEMS

Ask contractors what type of problems might happen. Experienced remodelers have a good idea of what to expect from a job. They can be of great help to you in the planning stage. If you address potential problems before they happen, you will lower your stress level during the job. Even with the best planning, unplanned incidents occur. Knowing how to deal with these problems is important. Quick decisions can turn into mistakes and disappointments. There will be very few problems that require an immediate answer. Avoid deciding on a solution without reflecting on the problem.

Contractors will want you to decide quickly. They don't want to pay their workers to stand around waiting for your answer. Remember, these contractors are working for you.

Maintain your power position and don't let them tell you what to do. Allow the contractors to make suggestions, but don't automatically accept their recommendations. The decision to accept their ideas without thinking them through can be very expensive. If you are paying for it, contractors will take the path of least resistance, regardless of cost. Don't hesitate to get additional opinions on decisions requiring major money. You could become a victim of a greedy contractor.

What type of snap decisions are you likely to face? Anything you can think of, and some things you can't imagine are possible. There are some problems that come up frequently. These are the ones we are going to concentrate on. If your job runs without any unexpected problems, it would probably be the first job to do so. Plan to encounter some obstacles during the course of your job.

> Stay in control. It's your house and your money; make your own informed decisions.

Remodeling is a business that revolves around accurate scheduling. An unkept commitment affects everybody. What happens when your electrician doesn't show up to rough in your electrical work? The first consequence is not having your electrical work done. The ripple effect is the need to reschedule all the other subcontractors. You will have to notify the insulation contractor of the delay. The drywall contractor will have to be postponed, and the painter will have to be rescheduled. The list continues to grow. One subcontractor can ruin your entire job schedule.

A strong contract will help to alleviate this problem. The subcontractor may still stiff you, but you will have recourse. You should have the ability to penalize him financially if your

> The most common problem in remodeling is unkept promises made by contractors or suppliers. When you have work scheduled and it doesn't go according to plan, you have several problems.

contract is worded properly. This threat will keep the job rolling. If it doesn't, exercise your contractual right to bring in a replacement subcontractor. Going over this information with each sub before the job begins will impress your intentions upon them. Let them know that time is critical and you can't afford down time. Be cordial but be firm, and don't give on this issue.

SUPPLIERS

Suppliers are harder to control than contractors. They can be undependable and bring your job to a dead stop. The hardest-working contractor can't operate without materials. Many times you will be promised delivery dates, which come and go with no material. This is a constant problem. When your remodeling crews can't work, they will go to another job where they can. They have to feed their families and must work to make money. You can't expect them to wait indefinitely for missing material. Once they leave your job, getting them back can be difficult.

You have to retain control over suppliers the same way you do with contractors. Here are some suggestions that may help when working with suppliers:

- When you place a material order, get the name of the individual taking the order and record it in a material log.

- Record the date and time you ordered the material.

- Record the delivery date you were promised.

- Call back the next day and ask the manager of the store to confirm your delivery date.

- Make written notes of this confirmation and get the manager's name.

- If delivery day comes and the material doesn't, go to see the manager. Go in person and take your log with you.

- Sit down with the manager and ask where your delivery is when the delivery is late.

- Use your material log as leverage.

- File a formal complaint against the supplier if necessary

Supplier-related problems cause the most trouble during remodeling. A special order that isn't placed could cost you six weeks in time. When completing your material order log, request order numbers. All special orders will have some type of order or reference number. When you are given these numbers, you have some proof that the order was placed. It is important to have material delivered before you need it. This gives you time to check the order before it's required. If something is missing, you have time to react before the job is interrupted. Plan ahead and check all orders closely. Compare the material order to the delivery ticket and check for backorders. If items are in boxes or crates, inspect them for damage. You don't want to wait until the plumber is ready to install your new tub to find out it is defective.

ON-THE-JOB PROBLEMS

On-the-job problems will happen. Anytime you are working with existing conditions, problems can be present. Animals can cause some of the worst and most unexpected problems. Over the years I've worked around animals many times. Your own pets are a potential problem that you may not have considered. You will need to make arrangements to allow workers to come and go in your house freely. Do not think you can ask contractors to take on the added responsibility of keeping your pet in the house. By the same token, provide any necessary protection to the contractor. Your lovable canine companion, who would never hurt a flea, may become confused or frightened by strange workers invading his home. I have seen many a placid puppy become a raging ball of claws and teeth.

The presence of wild animals is always an unwelcome surprise. I worked on a house inhabited by raccoons. These native inhabitants can create some interesting remodeling problems. Once when I was working on a house in the mountains, strange events started happening. The job had progressed to the finished drywall stage. The sheetrock was hung, and coated with the first coat of drywall compound.

The next day, there were holes in the walls. The first hole was around the water-supply pipe to the toilet. We thought the plumber had made a mistake and enlarged the hole to correct a problem. When confronted, the plumber denied knowing anything about the saucer-sized hole. We found the next hole in the ceiling of a closet. Later that day, I was downstairs with the painter when we heard a loud banging upstairs. Upon investigation, we were confronted by an angry Norway rat the size of a rabbit. Our construction had disturbed their domicile, and they were claiming homestead rights in the customer's house. This problem required a professional exterminator.

It isn't too unusual to find wild creatures living in and around rural homes. I've run into rattlesnakes, bats, and skunks. Is there any way to prepare for these unwanted neighbors? Contractors may find signs of wild animals if you require them to inspect your property before bidding the job. Bats are not difficult to detect; they leave quite a mess. Some animals will burrow under or into your home, and these holes may be found during an inspection. I once came face-to-face with a skunk family while crawling under a house to check existing conditions. Some animals can be removed without harm, and others will require more serious measures. You have to deal with each case independently.

When the insulating contractor comes out of your attic with bad news, sit down. Insulators can be the first people who have been in your attic for years. When they go up, they could come down with discouraging information. They may tell you about small piles of sawdust in your attic. These sawdust piles indicate wood-boring insects. These little creatures can do more damage than a beaver. These bugs are in the wood when the house is built, and under the right conditions they

Rotted lumber and termite damage are common problems that can alter your remodeling plans fast. If you were planning to attach to existing wood and find it's rotted, you have to make new arrangements. In the course of replacing your siding, you might discover decayed band boards or sills. These are very serious problems. You will need time to decide what course of action to take. Get several estimates and investigate all your options.

become active. They eat through your rafters and ceiling joists, which weakens your roof structure and calls for prompt, serious action.

The removal of these wood-infesting insects can be very expensive. If you are a victim of these brutal bugs, contact pest-control companies. Call several and request damage reports and extermination estimates. Some wood eaters can be stopped by treating the wood; others require a total fumigation of the house. The difference in cost is extensive. Be sure of the type of creature you are dealing with. Don't allow yourself to be sold a tented fumigation you don't need.

If you are remodeling a room upstairs, you can be in for some unexpected revelations. Suppoe that the remodeling work requires moving walls and installing new subflooring. You are sitting at your breakfast table, listening to the pounding and beating of the carpenters. You think how happy you are to be leaving in five minutes for work. When you come home, you go up to inspect the day's work. The carpenters made good progress, and everything looks acceptable.

You go downstairs to watch the evening news on television. When you sit back in your recliner, you notice spots on your family-room ceiling. A closer look reveals exposed nail heads. There are entire lines of them speckling your ceiling. The demolition work upstairs pushed the nail heads through the ceiling. Now you discover small spots of white powder on your carpet from the old drywall compound. What should you do now?

> Spend the time to make rational decisions. Call in professional building contractors to evaluate structural damage.

Call the carpentry contractor and explain what has happened. Ask when he is going to repair your ceiling. With the right language in your contract, this will be the contractor's problem. Your contract should include a clause regarding damage to existing conditions or other contractor's work. This clause specifies that damage done to your home or to another contractor's work is the responsibility of the contractor causing the damage. Including the right phrases in your contract will solve many problems before they happen.

QUICK DECISIONS

Quick decisions are dangerous. If you are at work, your mind isn't on remodeling. When your contractor calls you at work with a problem, you aren't in the best position to make a good decision. If the situation has to be dealt with immediately, consider the following options:

- Get all the information from the contractor and agree to call back in fifteen minutes. Fifteen minutes isn't a lot of time, but it will allow you the opportunity to think.

- Take a coffee break and review the circumstances.

- Decide if you should go home and see the problem. Many modest problems can be solved on short notice over the telephone.

- For complex problems take time to evaluate the alternatives.

- Use your own judgment but avoid immediate decisions whenever possible.

- When problems arise, don't panic.

- Allow enough time to settle down before making a decision.

- If the problem is expensive or complicated, wait until the next day to make your decision.

FEAR

Another common reaction is one of fear. Some problems are threatening. A lot of this has to do with the way the contractor presents the problem. Some contractors try to sell work using scare tactics. They hope you will decide immediately to correct the deficiency without shopping for prices. This approach is effective with many consumers. If the customer feels there is impending danger, he will act quickly and usually make a bad decision. This is why so many contractors rely on scare tactics for sales.

When you have a dangerous situation, don't make any decision that you don't have to until a code officer arrives. The inspector will be able to advise you of the nature of the problem and extent of the repairs needed. Once you know what needs to be done, get some quotes on the work. You are not obligated to hire the existing contractor to do the work. He should give you the best price, but he may try to take advantage of his

If you are presented with a problem involving possible danger, you should act quickly. You should call the local code office and request an emergency inspection. Before you actually call the code office, apprise the contractor of your plan to do so. The urgency of the repair may dissipate quickly. If the contractor is exaggerating, he will probably change his opinion when he learns the code officer will be coming, in response to his claim. If the contractor sticks to his story, you probably do have a real problem.

working relationship with you. Get other bids before awarding an expensive, unplanned job to the existing contractor. He won your original job with good prices, and he is already working on the job. Unless he is trying to take advantage of you, his prices should be competitive. If his price is competitive, let him do the job. Even if his price is a little higher, give him the work. You already know something about him and his work. This is an advantage over dealing with unknown contractors. Here are some common-sense solutions for unexpected problems:

- Common sense will get you through most on-the-spot decisions.
- The first rule is to try avoiding rash decisions.
- The second rule requires you to be fully informed.

- The third rule is to shop prices if it is an expensive decision.

- The fourth rule is to get everything in writing.

- If the existing contractor will be doing the work, use a change order.

- If a new contractor will be doing the work, complete a contract for the work.

Let's review the purpose of each rule. Avoiding rash decisions will protect you from mistakes made in haste. Any quick decision has the potential to be a bad decision. If you don't take the time to think, you are leaving yourself wide open. Full-time contractors develop an ability to make on-the-spot decisions through years of experience and mistakes. Their judgment has been honed to a sharp edge from years in the business.

As a homeowner, you don't have the experience to base quick answers on. This increases your risk of failure. Don't expect to be able to compete with the pros when it comes to quick decisions. Do the best you can. Take your time and make the best decision possible, using all the available information. The decision may cost you a little money, but you have already saved money by price shopping or running your own job. These are offsetting qualities. Don't worry about the small stuff; direct your attention the job's success.

The second rule is critical to a good on-the-spot decision. Your decision will be based on the information you have available to evaluate. The more information you have, the better your decision will be. Request all available information. When you have compiled the information, study it. With enough thought, the answer to the question will come to you. Stick to your first decision. If you start second-guessing yourself, you will regret it. Go with your gut instincts; they prevail in most circumstances.

If you are surprised with existing problems, take the time to gather quotes. This rule can be worth more money than all your efforts to this point. Sometimes the repairs can cost more than the original job. You shopped for contractors to do your job and you should shop for contractors to do your big repairs. Use the same techniques that you used to find the first contractors. Follow all the same rules and don't treat large repairs lightly. A dishonest contractor can take you for the financial ride of your life. If you don't question the prices, you will never know if you paid too much.

The fourth rule is one of the most important. Getting everything in writing is the golden rule. Never abandon it. Even if the repair is only a few hundred dollars, get it in writing. Without a written agreement, you could easily be facing a mechanic's lien. Any work done on your house could result in a lien. There is no need for this; if you put everything in writing, you eliminate unnecessary risks. Use change orders and all the other forms I have discussed. Repairs can cause you more trouble than the primary job.

You are now well informed on how to handle emergency situations. You should be able to recognize the difference between an inconvenience, a problem, and an emergency. You know what to do and how to do it. This information is valuable in all conditions. If you are your own contractor, the information is crucial. If you employ a general contractor, the information will help you meet the challenges and reduce your stress level. Snap decisions are an often-overlooked aspect of remodeling. Your new-found knowledge will protect you; it will shelter you from mistakes and save your bank account in an emergency. Now you can move ahead with your project with confidence.

12

The Punch-Out Process

T he end of the job is in sight. All that is left are minor adjustments and touch-ups. You have conquered the remodeling challenge and emerged victorious. The job has turned out wonderfully, and the small problems along the way are forgotten. Now you think that all you have left to do is enjoy the new improvements. Wrong—there are still many details to cover, and events can still go wrong. Don't ignore the final elements of your project. A common error is to get too lenient at the end of a project. Mistakes made at this point will cast a dark shadow on the entire job.

Your contractors are anxious to finish their work, get paid, and get on to the next job. In the rush to finish, accidents can happen. This is the time when most senseless problems occur. Toilets get broken, carpets get soiled, and walls get scraped by fixtures and appliances. The last few days of the job can be the most trying.

You've worked hard to get to this point. The vinyl flooring in your kitchen is perfect. The cabinets took weeks to get but are finally installed.

Tomorrow the plumber and the electrician are coming to finish their work. All your new fixtures and appliances will be working by the time you get home from work. You are excited and can't wait to try everything out.

When you come home the next day, your heart sinks. The first thing you see is a big gouge in your new kitchen floor. The vinyl is torn and wrinkled. At this moment nothing else matters. All you can think about is the ruined designer flooring. After several weeks with no major mishaps you thought you were out of the woods. Now your floor is torn. It's ripped in front of the dishwasher, most likely torn when the dishwasher was pulled out to be connected. The question is, who's responsible for the repair or replacement of the floor?

You know that either the plumber or the electrician is responsible, but you don't know which. They were the only trades in the house today. Both of them had connections to make to the dishwasher, and either one could have done the damage. After calling both contractors, neither will take the responsibility for the torn floor. What can you do? You can't blame both of them. Nobody was home to see which contractor tore the vinyl. You will probably have to absorb the cost of repairing the floor. How could this have been avoided?

There is no way for you to prevent a tear in the vinyl; these accidents happen. They shouldn't happen with experienced workers, but they can. Your mistake was in the way you scheduled your subcontractors. If the plumber had been working in the house alone, he would have to be the guilty party. You would have much more leverage under these conditions. It would be hard for the plumber to lie his way out of the situation if he was the only trade in the house that day.

> Throughout a job it is best to only have one trade on the job at a time.

Sometimes a contractor isn't aware that he caused damage and will flatly deny it. You might think anyone with any semblance of intelligence would know if he had torn your floor or scraped your walls. Cramped quarters lend themselves to unintentional damage. Putting several tradesmen to work in a small area spells trouble. They will not be as productive, and accidents are more likely to happen. They may not realize that while passing one another in the hall they scratched the wall with their tools. If you can't be on the job personally, careful scheduling is the best way to place proper blame for accidents.

> Pay particular attention to detail near the end of the job. If something is damaged, you need to know when it was damaged. If a problem is overlooked, you could be blaming the wrong contractor for the damage. Never underestimate the possible problems that can occur during the last week of the job. The tendency to relax will cause you unnecessary grief.

PUNCH LISTS

You will need to inspect all the finish work before giving final payment for the services rendered. This inspection should be done after all the contractors claim to be completely finished. As a result of a final inspection you will develop a punch-list. This list will include all the items that still need attention. You should make separate punch lists for each trade. Your punch-list form should be used as a guide when making your final inspections to help you know what to look for. It is crucial to get these punch-list deficiencies corrected before final payment is made.

Punch lists cover every aspect of a job. They deal with doors that don't shut properly and places where the paint needs to be touched-up. The adhesive labels and product markings should be removed from your floor and fixtures. Windows should open and lock easily, and any paint should be scraped from the glass. If you did landscaping, make sure the grass seed has started to grow. Check every phase carefully.

You should inspect the work twice before presenting the list to the contractor. Conduct your first inspection in natural light. Open the drapes and go over the job

> It is much easier to have the contractor fix his mistakes before final payment is made.

under optimum daylight conditions. Then repeat the same inspection with artificial light in the evening. The type and amount of light will affect the appearance of the completed work. Fixture colors will appear differently in incandescent and fluorescent light. They look even more dissimilar in natural light. The same is true of paint colors.

PAINTERS

Painters have been known to use less expensive paints of similar colors to the up-graded choices they charged the customer for. Homeowners have been known to misjudge the appearance of colors they picked from small paint chips. Is there any way to verify that the painter used the correct paint? Yes, you can require him to leave any left-over paint. This is not unreasonable, since you paid for the paint and can use it for future touch-ups. If the product is in the original container, you can easily verify that it is the correct paint. If the paint is in large, unmarked buckets, your only other option is to have a sample from the paint store. When you pick-out the paint for your project, request samples of the colors on pieces of wall and trim board. Stain colors look differently on various types of wood and should be applied to the type of trim you will use. These procedures should eliminate surprise results at the end of the job and help to keep the contractor honest as well.

FLOORING

Flooring choices are made from small samples. The actual carpet or vinyl can look very different once it is installed. Expect to find some minor differences in the installed products. If the differences are drastic, compare the product numbers on the contract with the products installed. Confirm that you got what you paid for. If the wrong product was installed, you want to find out now. There is still time to have the problem resolved before final payment is issued. Although you may decide not to have the entire carpet torn out and replaced, you can certainly require restitution for accepting the wrong product. Check the carpet and vinyl installation for ripples and lumps. Seams should be invisible and all necessary thresholds in place before the flooring job is considered complete.

DRYWALL

Drywall work frequently I found on punch lists. Good drywall finishers are rare. If possible, try to look for drywall imperfections after the painter applies the first coat of primer. Catching a problem at this point will eliminate the need to repaint repaired areas later. It is especially important to inspect drywall under various lighting conditions. If you look at the job in natural light, it can look fine. You pay the contractor and he leaves. Incandescent light from your lamps will amplify a poor drywall job. When you look at the workmanship in the evening, you may find ripples and bad seams on your ceiling. If you signed a certificate of completion and satisfaction, you're stuck with the work.

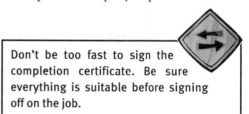

Don't be too fast to sign the completion certificate. Be sure everything is suitable before signing off on the job.

FIXTURES AND APPLIANCES

Personally test all your new fixtures and appliances. Here are some examples of what to check in a typical job:

- Electricians can forget to wire fixtures.

- Your new dishwasher may not run. It looks nice, but it doesn't work.

- Are the circuits in your electrical box marked correctly?

- If the circuit breaker is labeled for the water heater, it should control the water heater. Suppose that in the future you need to repair the water heater. If you throw an improperly labeled breaker, it will quite literally be a real shock.

- Electrical items are rarely checked, but they should be.

- If a new or additional heat source was installed, turn it on and make certain that it works. Don't wait until freezing temperatures to discover a faulty thermostat.

- Test everything yourself.

- Go into your new bathroom and gently rock the toilet; is it secured properly?

- Have the drop-in lavatory bowls and tub been caulked?

- Examine the water connections under bath and kitchen sinks and at the toilet tank for leaks.

- Fill your sinks and tubs with water; let the water out and make sure the drains work properly and do not leak.

- Don't assume everything is acceptable just because the contractor told you the work passed the final code inspection.

- Were all the required code-enforcement inspections actually completed?

- Ask for copies of the approved inspections, and don't make final payment until you have them.

- If the project is large, a certificate of occupancy is required before you can inhabit the new space. The certificate of occupancy will not be issued until all other inspections are completed and approved. Without the certificate of occupancy, the code officer can prohibit you from using your new space. Be sure to have this certificate before making any final payments.

- Have you looked under your new addition?

- Is the crawl space insulated?

- Did the contractors leave scrap wood on the ground under your addition?

- Don't ignore what you can't easily see.

- Inspect every aspect of the work done.

- Crawl spaces aren't attractive places, but you need to inspect them. Scrap wood left on the ground can encourage termite infestation. The insulation may have been omitted from the crawl space simply because a worker didn't think about it. As a consumer, you have to think about it. If you are paying for a vapor barrier, make sure it was installed. A quick crawl under the addition can reveal a lot. Contractors don't expect you to go into these areas. If they are intentionally going to let something slide, this is where they will do it.

- Check existing areas of your home, which may have been affected during the remodeling project.

- If workers were in your attic, make sure your insulation is undisturbed.

- Check your ceilings, carpets, walls, and floors.

- Look closely for scratches, cracks, and cigarette burns. If your contract was worded correctly, you will not have to accept these damages. If repairs need to be made to existing sections of your home, list these on a punch list as well.

Using a sample punch list as a guide, you will be able to conduct a good inspection. The sample will prompt you about the kind of items to inspect. When you are done, meet with the contractors and go over the punch lists. Explain what you found and how you want it corrected. This shouldn't be a problem with a strong contract as your shield. A good remodeling contract will clearly deal with punch lists. When the corrections have been made, inspect the work again. Check all the items just as thoroughly this time. Look for problems that may have been caused by correcting the items on your original punch list. Use the same procedures. If everything is all right, you can sign-off on the job.

Before making your final payments, there are few more chores to take care of. Here are some examples:

- Has the job been cleaned up to your satisfaction? If not, get it done now.

- Once you sign off and give final payment, what you see is what you get.

- Request all the owner's manuals and warranty cards before making final disbursements. You might be surprised how often these items can't be produced. Contractors are notorious for trashing these documents; don't let them get away with it. You need the owner's manual and warranty cards. If the contractor doesn't have them, make him get new ones.

- If you don't have the contractor's warranty period included in your contract, get it in writing now. This should have been in your contract; it's easier to cover this in the beginning than in the end. Most remodelers warranty their work for one year. Product warranties vary, depending on the manufacturer. If you have questions about the warranties, get them answered before final payment.

RETAINER

With all this behind you, the final payment is the next step. Are you allowed to retain money for problems? Smart contractors will want you to sign a certificate of completion and acceptance. The form basically states your acceptance of all work done and your satisfaction with the quality of the work. For such a small form, the consequences are great. Don't sign this form until you are completely satisfied with every aspect of the work. Once you verify your satisfaction of the work, the contractor is off the hook.

Often everything works fine on the final inspection. A week later there may be minor leaks in the compression fittings of your plumbing, or a light may begin to flicker. This happens all the time. There is a break-in period, and as you use some items, they may need minor adjustments. Most contractors will come back to take care of these adjustments, but some can be very difficult about putting more time into your job. If you are holding a cash retainer, the odds of getting the contractor back improve dramatically.

Retainers are usually not more than 10 percent of the final payment. This isn't a lot, but it does offer some motivation for the contractor to return. You can't hold a retainer unless it was agreed to in your contract. Your written agreement with the contractor is the backbone of your job. It details everything and reduces confusion. When properly composed, it also

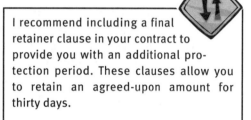

I recommend including a final retainer clause in your contract to provide you with an additional protection period. These clauses allow you to retain an agreed-upon amount for thirty days.

gives you leverage and protection. If a contractor refuses to correct a problem, at least you have some money set aside to pay someone else to make the repairs. You can even pay yourself to fix the problem if you are able to do the work. Seriously consider including a detailed retainer clause in your contracts. This little stratagem can eliminate hours of frustration.

CALL-BACKS

With or without retainers, call-backs are a bother. No contractor is going to want to come back and fix something for nothing. They got paid for what they did, and call-backs are a fact of life. Warranties and retainers obligate contractors to fix the problem, but they still will not want to come back. Although contractors know, sooner or later, that they will have to respond to your complaint, many will try to make it later rather than sooner. This can be extremely frustrating for you.

Call-backs are a part of warranty work. When something doesn't function properly, the contractor is called back to fix it.

Nobody likes call-backs. The customer doesn't appreciate having to request repairs on recently installed work, and contractors don't like correcting their mistakes for free. It would be wonderful if there were no need for call-backs. Unfortunately, the need is there and call-backs are a part of remodeling. The best you can hope for is a cooperative contractor.

From the contractors perspective, they hope for a reasonable homeowner. It is impossible to guarantee that there will be no problems with a remodeling project. All contractors are going to make mistakes. There will be circumstances beyond their control. Although using experienced tradesmen may reduce problems, it doesn't assure a lack of call-backs. The best remodelers available will still get an occasional call-back. Reputable contractors will respond to your request for call-back service promptly. Realistically, they should respond to call-backs quicker than new work. Your job is done and paid for. If you are having a problem, they should respond promptly. Unfortunately, this attitude is not universal.

Your call-back is not a paying job, so you no longer have any leverage. The contractor has your money and is in no hurry to rush back to your job. Is there anything you can do? You can try to stress the value of a favorable referral to the contractor. He should be concerned with customer relations, reputation, and good business practices. Whether he is or not is a different story. When call-backs arise, retainages may have already been paid. What can you do if the contractor won't respond to your requests? Without your financial leverage, do you have any effective options? Good contractors will respond quickly. It's the marginal or bad ones you have to worry about.

A lot of contractors put call-backs at the bottom of their priority list. They go to new work first because these jobs are generating fresh income. The contractor figures you can wait; he already has your money. This is the wrong attitude. You paid your final payment, and you are entitled to what you paid for. If you have a problem, you should be taken care of before a new project. Too many contractors are only interested in cash flow and ignore your request for warranty service.

If your original contract addressed warranty work, you

have an advantage. You have a written instrument, signed by the contractor, guaranteeing warranty work. This contract can still be used as a threat. If the contractor won't respond to your call, play your contract card. Explain to the contractor that you only want what was promised in the contract. If he still balks, get mean!

Threaten to sue the contractor for breach of contract. Advise him of your intention to file formal complaints with every available agency controlling contractor's licenses. Some agencies to name are:

- Code-enforcement office
- State licensing agency
- The Better Business Bureau
- The Chamber of Commerce

This may sound ruthless or extreme, but if the contractor is jerking you around, you have to regain some leverage. You shouldn't have to be subjected to this kind of treatment. You upheld your end of the contract; make the contractor uphold his part of your agreement.

The completion of the job should be a joyous day. You have successfully executed a complicated task. You saved money and still got everything you wanted. This provides a warm feeling of relief and happiness. You avoided the pitfalls and traps. You beat the odds. Now you can truly enjoy the results of your efforts. With the successful completion of your project, you deserve a reward. Whether you engaged a general contractor or ran the job yourself, the result is a completed, successful job.

INSURANCE

If everything went right, your house has a higher market value now. The replacement cost of the home has increased, which dictates a call to your insurance agent. It will be necessary to increase your insurance coverage. When you call your insurance agent, remember to allow for new furnishings. If you added space, you will most likely add personal belongings. These belongings should be added to your insurance policy. A new insurance inventory should be done; your old inventory will be outdated. Providing photos of your new improvements and furnishings will create a highly accurate insurance inventory. This will make your life easier if you have to file a claim.

Many big insurance claims involve fires or fallen trees. You did a good job contracting your addition, but if it is heavily damaged by fire, you are not the best person to contract the repairs. Fire jobs require highly specialized talent. They cannot be considered remodeling jobs. Fire jobs are in a class by themselves, and fire-related work will test a remodeler's mettle.

When you give the insurance agent figures for the value of the improvements, use retail figures, not your cost. If a disaster requires you to replace the improvements, you may not want to do it yourself. Allow enough insurance coverage to hire professionals.

Estimating the repair costs is very difficult. There is a lot more to these jobs than meets the eye.

Fire jobs present nasty working conditions. You don't always know how extensive the smoke and water damage is. This is no place for a part-timer. If you are contemplating contracting your own fire job, forget it. You must have extensive experience to be qualified to do the job. The average contractor isn't qualified either. If you are dealing with a fire job, find a specialist. Fire jobs are no place for novices.

THE END

When you approach the end of your project, you will be elated. There will be a strong sense of pride. When you started planning your job, you had little or no experience. You mustered the courage to face intimidating odds, and everything has turned out fine. Now you can't understand why people make such a fuss over remodeling.

Your personal experience has proved the horror stories wrong. This was a time-consuming project, but it wasn't too difficult.

Reaching a successful completion was a matter of education and self-discipline. You studied your options before beginning the process. This knowledge guided you to a successful conclusion. Your discipline allowed you to stick to the remodeling rules. The rules helped you avoid the pitfalls and gave you a good template to follow. The money you saved is substantial. All in all, this was a rewarding and pleasurable experience. There were no miracles or magic needed to orchestrate the project. It only required a clear head and sensible decisions.

Where do all the bad stories come from? They are originated by uninformed consumers. These homeowners don't expend the same energy or research their actions the way you did. For the unprepared self-contractor, remodeling can be a less than desirable experience. You should be proud; you've almost made it to the finish line. You made the right decisions. You learned how to make the most of your abilities. By taking an active interest in the job, you can appreciate the work that went into it. This was not an effortless responsibility. What will you do with the money you saved? You can put it in the bank or treat yourself to a celebration. A good plan is to do a little of both.

Don't take your work hat off yet. Invest some of your savings and treat yourself to some goodies for your efforts. Allow yourself some rewards for your hard work. In the next chapter, we are going to talk about interior decorating. This offers a valuable way to spend some of your savings. These expenditures will amplify the effects of your new space. Your choices in decorating will allow the opportunity to get the most from your remodeling project. The right moves with interior choices will personalize your remodeling efforts.

This is where you put your personality into your house. All the heavy work is done. The house is beginning to look more like a home and less like a construction site. You are done with the stress of managing the crews and suppliers. All that is left is the fun of adding your special accessories. This final stage of the remodeling process will be meaningful and enjoyable.

Index

Page numbers in italics refer to figures and tables